5.
5/22

A Wild Ride:

Bears, Babes and Marketing to the Max

Ed Lewi
with Paul Grondahl

A Wild Ride:
Bears, Babes and Marketing to the Max

Ed Lewi with Paul Grondahl

Published by Lulu 2014.
Copyright © Ed Lewi 2014

ISBN # 978-1-312-37242-9

Printed in U.S.A.

Cover photo by Barney Fowler:
Ed riding in a convertible in the early 1960s with a black
bear and Maureen. He started working in 1954 for The
Great Escape. Ed's philosophy: "If it's not fun, don't do it."

All photographs from Ed Lewi's collection and
used with permission.

Book design: Carin Lane

Contents:

Foreward:
Marylou Whitney & John Hendrickson

E d Lewi is the Maestro! It does not matter if Ed is working on public relations, donating his efforts to charity or just enjoying time with friends, Ed always has to be the ringleader. We have watched Ed work his magic on numerous events and situations for over 40 years and there is one constant ingredient: FUN!

Ed has many success stories, but the best chapter in his life is the day he met his wife, Maureen. Ed is fortunate to have a partner and a soul mate who has translated all his ideas into action. Over the years, many friends have remarked that when Maureen married Ed she not only had to sign the marriage certificate, but also a work permit. Every one of Ed's ideas requires many working hours and much organization to see them come to fruition. The Maestro's partner has always been the go-to person to get things done. Maureen, a perfectionist by nature, also shares Ed's passion for fun. She has been a tireless advocate for many organizations, but none more important than Ed. It is a well-known fact that Ed Lewi would not be alive today if it weren't for Maureen!

A charitable gentleman by nature, Ed was born to be a leader in making things around him better. He is not happy unless he has 100 different things going on in his life. Many charities, businesses and people around the Capital Region have prospered tremendously because of Ed's hard work and philosophy. The Saratoga Race Course, the Saratoga Performing Arts Center, the Double H Ranch and Camp Chingachgook – to name a few – would not be the institutions they are today without the wisdom and energy of Ed Lewi.

Over the years we have become best friends with Ed and Maureen. We seem to gravitate toward their company because of their love of giving and love of laughter. We cannot imagine better friends.

As you read this book, we hope you enjoy Ed's life as much as he has enjoyed living it!

Introduction:
Life's a Party

Long Lake N.Y. 7/36

Adventurous even at age 3, Ed paddles his own canoe on Long Lake, the start of a lifelong connection to the Adirondacks.

I was born seven weeks prematurely. Maybe that explains why I've always been a hustler. I couldn't wait to get some skin in the game. Even as a preemie, I was a husky kid. For as long as I can remember, I've had a big appetite for life. You could say I was born hungry. Let me explain. My mom had been at home in Schenectady, roasting a turkey, on New Year's Eve, 1933. She also had another one in the oven, namely me, and I guess I was in a hurry to get out into the world even though it was a tough time economically. The Great Depression was stubbornly hanging on and still causing a lot of despair, but my

mom and dad weren't going to let an economic crisis ruin their tradition of throwing a big party to ring in the New Year. Instead of hosting her popular New Year's Eve party that year, though, my mom went into early labor and I was delivered at around 6 p.m. on December 31 — just in time to be declared a tax deduction, my dad liked to remind me.

My arrival was totally unexpected and I had obviously scotched my folks' party plans. So much for my mom's idea of serving turkey at her party. I arrived and I was 100% ham from the get-go.

I could blame the ham factor on my

A photo of Ed's father, Joe Lewi, with women trying on fur coats. Joe quit school at age 13 and went to work for the Carl Co. He started as a maintenance worker there and ended up as a vice president who started several new departments. He later opened his own high-end retail store and became a well-known business and civic leader in Schenectady. The Lewi Co. was a very successful business that Joe left to his wife upon his death at age 54. Ed worked the business with his mom, Sadie, but his interests were in a part-time job that he held at the Schenectady Gazette in the sports department. On Saturdays, the busiest retail day, Ed went missing from the store and was out covering football games. Ed had no interest in retail.

dad, Joe Lewi, a first-class schmoozer himself. In my father, I was blessed with a marvelous teacher when it came to walking softly and carrying a big shtick.

To get back to the story of my birth, there was my mother, Sadie Lewi, cradling me in the labor and delivery room at Ellis Hospital and fretting about the turkey roasting in the oven and all the food she had prepared and left in a hurry back at our house when my dad rushed her to the hospital. As it happened, the obstetrician who delivered me was a social acquaintance of my parents and they had invited him to their New Year's Eve house party. But he was otherwise occupied at Ellis Hospital, of course, as was my mother. My mom, a real trouper, didn't let my premature birth get in the way of her party plans. Being a practical sort, she wouldn't hear of wasting all that fine food she had spent the day preparing, so she dispatched my dad to go home and bring the turkey and the rest of the party spread to the hospital. Despite the fact that she had just given birth, Sadie decided she would have her New Year's Eve party, after all, only in the maternity ward. It was a movable feast.

Ever since the hospital party I hosted as a newborn, I've always enjoyed grand entrances. I've made a nice career out of staging dramatic promotional moments and professional hijinks as president one of the oldest and most successful public relations firms in the Capital Region, Ed Lewi Associates. Much of the credit for our firm's success, of course, goes to my multi-talented and long-suffering wife, Maureen. She not only encouraged and supported my inner zaniness, she helped me to learn at least a modicum of restraint and to choose more judiciously when to unleash the outrageous P.R. stunts and old-fashioned

razzle-dazzle for which I became something of an infamous local legend

"I knew when to rein him in," Maureen says. Truer words were never spoken.

Members of the working media loved my wild and crazy promotions and came to expect the unexpected with me. They never failed to show up with a smile on their faces and a gleam in their eyes when I produced one of my promotional extravaganzas. The press turned out in spades when I coaxed Marylou Whitney, the Queen of Saratoga and doyenne of the city's social scene, to ride an elephant for her entrance to promote the opening of the Saratoga Performing Arts Center. Marylou's a dear friend of mine and a good sport and she endured the pachyderm parade with panache and, fortunately, no problems.

It's been called the media circus, of course, and I considered myself a ringmaster to the fun. Animals were my specialty. Over the years, I worked with a trained bear and got the beast to hawk Times Union newspapers. Some old-timers still talk about that stunt I put together in downtown Albany. It's never a dull moment when we bring in lions and tigers and bears, oh my. I even talked Maureen, whom I was dating at the time, into posing for a photograph with a playful lion. She's been putting up with my outrageous and original ideas for P.R. and promotions ever since. It's definitely been a wild ride. We've worked with plenty of celebrities along the way, too. You can blame it all on my mom. She threw a big party to ring in the New Year a few short hours after my birth. Life's been a party ever since. I've had so much fun along the way it should have been declared illegal. View these photographs, read the stories that go with them and enjoy the wild and crazy ride. We sure did.

This photo was taken in 1949 when Ed was an assistant cook at Camp Chingachgook. He began as a camper at age 7 in 1940 and has enjoyed a 70+ year association, from lifeguard, to exploratory leader to Chairman of the Board of Directors for 12 years. The dining hall and administration office building is named Lewi Lodge in recognition of the $10 million Ed has raised for the YMCA Camp on Lake George.

Chapter 1:
Paul Newman, A Kid at Heart

Paul Newman shares a private moment with Ed at a Double H Ranch fundraising event in Saratoga Springs.

Everyone was excited over the visit by Paul Newman to the Double H Ranch, a Hole in the Wall Gang camp for critically ill children on Lake Luzerne in the Adirondacks. The property had been a dude ranch before it was purchased by my close friend, mentor and client, Charles R. "Charley" Wood, the Lake George amusement park impresario and philanthropist. Paul and Charley were co-founders of the Double H Ranch.

We joined board members and a few spouses for Paul's arrival at the camp. Paul sidestepped the assembled grown-ups and headed right for the terminally ill children to whom he is devoted.

A few moments later, he looked over the tops of his glasses with those mesmerizing, sapphire-blue eyes that launched a million swooning female fans and whispered an aside to me: "You're in the P.R. business, right? I've got a job for you. Please explain to the adults that I will be sitting with the kids." I did so.

It was a delight on that visit and several others to watch Paul's genuine warmth and love of the kids. He was low-key, down-to-earth and in no way impressed with his own celebrity. He didn't want reporters or photographers around. He just wanted to connect directly with the sick kids. He brought smiles to their faces when he joined in with their songs and games at lunch and was always a good sport, no matter what the children asked him to do. There was a camp rule that banned elbows from resting on the table and if someone was caught breaking the rule, the penalty was that they had to run around the camp's dining hall before they could sit back down and eat their meal. Trying to catch each other forgetting and resting elbows on the table was great sport and the campers erupted with cheers and laughter when someone had to run around the building outside.

I'll never forget watching the kids "catch" Paul when he had supposedly forgotten and rested his elbows on the table and they were giddy with getting to "call" him on his gaffe. Without missing a beat, he nodded his head, indicating he was guilty as charged, stood up and trotted off toward the dining hall door. He ran out into a torrential downpour and sprinted around the entire building as kids pressed their noses to windows to watch and cheer. The Academy Award-winning actor and American icon came back inside, winded and dripping wet, with a big grin on his famously handsome face. He would do anything to entertain these seriously ill kids and help them feel better, at least for a time.

Paul was the most generous, charitable and well-meaning person I have known. I never saw him perform his good deeds or philanthropy for anything but the right reasons. He helped others and made the world a better place because he enjoyed lifting others up. It actually made my work more difficult because he shunned publicity, awards and accolades for his charitable work. I had the privilege of seeing his executive decision-making and business acumen from the inside and he was simply brilliant in that regard. But what endeared him to so many of us was that he never seemed interested in impressing others in the slightest. He knew who he was, what he was about and he was comfort-able in his own skin. There was no pretense about Paul. Most of the time when I met with him, he wore beat-up sneakers, well-worn khakis, a sweatshirt and sunglasses. He enjoyed a cold bottle of beer in his hand, never bothering with a glass.

Whenever he came to the North Country, Paul always insisted that he be seated at lunch or dinner next to Maureen. They had a special relationship. He appreciated that she wasn't star-struck and didn't go all weak-kneed and googly-eyed over his fame and legendary good looks. What he treasured most about Maureen was her candid remarks and keen sense of observation. The two of them huddled at meals and Paul pumped Maureen for all the latest gossip and her honest opinions. She obliged. He frequently laughed over their joint observations and shared opinions. He was pretty verbal about his personal opinions with Maureen, as opposed to his public persona.

Paul didn't get bogged down in all the usual B.S. and diva behavior common to celebrities. He didn't play mind games and preferred if you cut right to the chase. I remember one meeting I attended with Paul and Charley. The first thing Paul liked to do when he arrived at Double H Ranch was to look over the books and review the financial records. He had a brilliant mind for business and he'd immediately zero in on any problems within minutes of scanning the records. And when it came down to closing a deal, he didn't dither. I remember one meeting that Charley had spent weeks preparing for and Paul wrapped it up in no more than ten seconds. We sat down at a conference table and here's how the meeting went.

Paul: "How much do you guys want?"

Charley: "A million dollars."

Paul: "OK."

That was it. The meeting was over. We all stood up and went to lunch.

Paul and Charley got to know each other after Charley read an article about Paul's Hole in the Wall Gang Camp in the New York Times. Charley wrote to the famous actor offering to help him found a camp for critically ill kids in Lake George. Unfortunately, the relationship between them grew strained after Charley began to suffer what appeared to be the early stages of Alzheimer's disease. Charley was in his 80s by then, his mental capacities had declined and his behavior had become erratic. Paul made two special trips to meet with Charley, who quit the Board of Directors and took a "leave of absence" from the operations of the Double H Ranch in the fall of 1999. I was Vice Chairman and Paul kept me and the other members of the Executive Committee informed about his efforts to appease Charley. The talks broke down and Paul felt his efforts had become futile. He reached me by phone at a hotel in Cody, Wyoming where Maureen and I were staying. He told me bluntly that for the good of the organization and the kids we had to move on without Charley. We hated to do so, but we had no alternative because we had to fix a crippling $900,000 deficit without wasting any more time. Paul told me he was prepared to offer the Ranch a "bridge loan" in that amount, essentially erasing the deficit.

I guess I was slightly naïve, because I became concerned about how much interest we would be charged and I was worried that we wouldn't be able to generate enough cash flow to pay the loan back and we would face a bigger deficit and perhaps penalties.

Paul listened quietly as I rambled on. He was calm and paused before he said in that famous low, gravelly voice:

"The bridge goes nowhere, Ed."

I guess I was a little dense. It took a few moments for Paul's grace and generosity to sink in for me. Then, I suddenly understood.

The guy was pure class. Like I said, I never knew anybody more genuinely kind and generous than Paul.

Paul gives Maureen a kiss on the cheek during the charity event. The famous actor was warm and caring to the critically ill children he visited regularly at the Double H Ranch, which he co-founded with philanthropist Charley Wood.

Chapter 2:
The Golden Bear

Legendary golfer Jack Nicklaus and Ed met at the Lake Placid Club during negotiations with golf resort developer Gleneagles to hire "The Golden Bear" to re-design the course. The project was abandoned after it met resistance from the Adirondack Park Agency.

I hate to acknowledge missed opportunities when it comes to my beloved Lake Placid, but the Adirondack Park Agency (APA) really blew it when it came to a terrific chance to improve and re-energize the Lake Placid Club, the community's flagship resort and golf course, a few years after the 1980 Winter Olympics.

Gleneagles, the premier golf resort developer in the British Isles (under corporate owner Guinness), partnered with American insurance giant USF&G and were prepared to invest significant sums to renovate the famous Lake Placid Club, the anchor of the Adirondack alpine town since it was founded in 1907 by library innovator Melvill Dewey. The Lake Placid Club enjoyed a tremendous reputation as a world-class resort and golf course during the 1932 Olympics and had its heyday from the 1940s to the 1970s. But by the time the Olympics returned in 1980, the facility had fallen into severe disrepair. The Gleneagles and USF&G

consortium, with the backing of Gleneagles corporate owner Guinness, wanted to restore the resort's past luster and hired me to help them with public relations – as recommended by their attorney Jim Brooks, who initially didn't want me in Lake Placid after my botched interview, but who became a good friend and valued advisor during the Winter Olympics.

When Gleneagles brought in golfing legend Jack Nicklaus, known as the "Golden Bear" and the greatest player in the history of the game, I figured we were on a fast track to restore the Lake Placid Club to its rightful place as a first-class destination. Nicklaus visited the property and re-designed the golf course with a gentle touch and reverence for the region's history. In the end, he proposed major alterations on only two holes, mainly to improve drainage and eliminate run-off without changing the look of the course or the surrounding views.

Despite all their care and the major investments planned on their proposed re-development, the APA shut down the Gleneagles folks cold. They refused to issue any of the necessary permits and blocked the plan at every turn. I remember being very impressed with Jack Nicklaus during our meetings. He was all business and very polite and he sat through the shabby treatment he received at APA hearings without losing his temper or voicing complaint.

But Lake Placid needed Nicklaus and the Gleneagles folks more than they needed Lake Placid. In the end, the investors, tired of encountering resistance by the APA, simply abandoned the plan. They pulled up stakes and took their money and know-how to Manchester, Vermont, where they worked with the receptive folks at the Equinox resort and re-developed that golf course into a first-class layout and golfing complex that draws tourists from around the world.

It was a major loss for Lake Placid and I was outraged that the APA could shut down the Gleneagles folks that way. It was a blown opportunity and we lost the chance to make the Lake Placid Club once again a world-class golf course and resort destination. Meeting Nicklaus was a highlight for me, but the outcome left a sour taste in my mouth and was one of the major disappointments during my long association with Lake Placid.

***

Chapter 3:
Dancing with the Stars

When Ed joined the Saratoga Performing Arts Center board, he hosted a welcome back parade down Broadway for the New York City Ballet. Pictured at the parade, from left, Saratoga Springs Mayor Michael Lenz; Ed; SPAC Executive Director Marcia White; SPAC Chairman William Dake; former NYCB principal dancer Darci Kistler; her husband, Peter Martins, NYCB Ballet Master in Chief and their daughter, Talicia.

I owe my dancing career at the Saratoga Performing Arts Center to legendary New York City Ballet founder George Balanchine and a "lift" I received from Mr. B's protégé, Peter Martins. My balletic star turn did have some unintended catastrophic consequences. Luckily, they never made me wear a tutu and pointe shoes.

Let me set the scene. I was taking members of the European press on a backstage tour of SPAC, when we walked in on a class of NYCB dancers being led by the great Balanchine He couldn't have been pleased with my

interruption, but he decided to have a little fun with me. He proposed to give me a dancing lesson and asked me to approach the barre along the wall. He told me to raise my leg to the barre. I tried to oblige, but as I got my leg halfway up to the waist-high rail, I heard a sickly sound, a crunching and grinding noise. My ballet debut landed me in the hospital with a ruptured disc.

My dancing disaster only deepened my reverence for Mr. B., whom I saw frequently as he strolled the hilly driveway from the SPAC amphitheater, dressed impeccably with his ascot and dramatic pocket scarf, accompanied by two corps ballerinas, one on each arm, as he tutored the talented hopefuls sacrificing and working their way to become principal dancers with the famous NYCB.

Another golden moment during our 15 years handling public relations for SPAC occurred when ballet legend Martins, the impossibly handsome Dane, decided it was time we did a pas de deux. I valued my friendship with Peter, one of the most talented and popular principal dancers ever to grace the SPAC stage. We also got to know each other at the Saratoga Race Course, where I often bumped into him placing bets at the $50 window. He knew a lot about horse racing and didn't mind giving me tips on the horses he liked.

Among all the acclaim and honors and rave reviews Peter Martins achieved during his many years at SPAC, nothing compares to his extraordinary achievement with yours truly. The incident occurred during a celebratory parade Maureen and I organized that traversed the city and wound up at the Canfield Casino as part of a celebration after the NYCB announced that it was returning to SPAC for a long-term commitment after it had considered ending it's summer residency in Saratoga. I was immersed in details of the parade when I felt two powerful arms wrap me in a bear hug from behind and lift me – I tipped the scales at over 200 pounds at that point – several feet off the ground. It was Peter Martins. He held me up there for what seemed like minutes, the way he had lifted so many famous ballerinas over the years. Then he placed me gently back on the ground, burst out in a laugh and gave me a slap on the shoulder. It was just Peter being Peter. Luckily, my back had recovered from my Mr. B. catastrophe and Peter's lift didn't result in another disc injury. After he lifted me, I realized that Peter was a real heavyweight in dance.

***

Chapter 4:

Breakfast with the Kennedy's

Ed was working as a stringer photographer for the Associated Press and ended up plucking Caroline Kennedy, center, from a river in the Adirondacks at North Creek after she fell near the dock on a canoe trip with her uncle Bobby, left, and cousin, Courtney, right.

It was a big story for the local media when Bobby Kennedy took his family on a vacation in the Adirondack Mountains. I was working as an advertising salesman at the Times Union at the time and moonlighting as a fill-in freelance photographer for the Associated Press. I was friends with several of the wire service shooters and they sometimes called on me when their regular staffers were busy and they needed an event covered. This was one of those occasions. Since the AP didn't' have a "real photographer," they decided to dispatch me as a last resort to photograph the Kennedys in the North Country. The term was "stringer," which gives you a sense of how my photography skills were regarded.

My assignment was to try go get a few shots of the Kennedys whitewater rafting in the upper Hudson River near North Creek. They weren't expecting a lot out of me. The Kennedy camp put out word that there would be no press allowed in the launching area for the rafting trip at the Gooley Club, a private hunting preserve in North Creek. I didn't have much pressure on me at first, until I was informed that I was being teamed up with Pulitzer Prize-winning photographer Eddie Adams. This was in 1970 and Adams had recently returned from the Vietnam War with a stunning collection of iconic images. The AP assigned Eddie and told him he would be meeting an "expert on the trail" for the assignment. Yikes, they were referring to me. Now, I felt myself getting weak in the knees. What expertise did I have to show the famous wartime photographer?

When I rendezvoused with Eddie in North Creek, I said I had scoped out a three-mile trail, through thick woods, that would bring us to the Kennedy launch site while eluding security.

I hiked in with Eddie and at the end of our vigorous hike, lugging logs of heavy photo gear, Eddie pulled out his huge 300 mm telephoto lens, zoomed in across the river, and asked me who the photographer was who was standing next to Senator Bobby Kennedy. I took a look through the lens and saw my old buddy, Joe Paeglow, chief photographer in Albany for United Press International. AP and UPI were competitors. Eddie muttered some choice words and I could tell he wanted to ditch me, and fast.

That's when my day took a turn into Murphy's Law territory. Eddie said he wanted me to head in the other direction to get a few shots of RFK with JFK's daughter Caroline and his daughter Courtney. Caroline and Courtney, who were 13 and 14 years old, respectively. Eddie moved out quickly to position himself to get the money shots of the Kennedys blasting through the Hudson's whitewater rapids. I schlepped my way back to the whitewater rafting finish area and sweet-talked my way through a maze of security. It helped that I had an in with the State Police, since I had been doing P.R. and taking photos for the troopers' organization. By the time I reached the dock, Senator Kennedy

was helping his nieces get out of the raft and back onto solid ground.

I went to work and was snapping some pictures when young Caroline somehow because distracted and miscalculated the wide step between the raft and the dock. In a split-second, she fell into the choppy waters of the river. I instinctively dropped my camera, and pulled her out of the cold river. Immediately, two Secret Service agents grabbed me. Ethel Kennedy materialized at my side, yelled at the agents, ordered them to let me go and praised my rescue of her frightened niece. She was furious with the Secret Service, first for letting Caroline fall in the water and second for treating me like some sort of criminal after I had pulled her out. Ethel was an angry aunt and she chewed out the agents but good.

Someone wrapped Caroline in blankets and led her away. The Kennedys were staying at the Garnet Hill Lodge and aides took the girls to the lodge to get warm. The senator and his wife came over to me and expressed their thanks in a very warm and genuine way and we talked about being parents and the trials and tribulations of child-raising. By the time we ended our conversation, we looked around and determined that all the vehicles of the Kennedy's entourage had left and Bobby and Ethel didn't have a ride back to Garnet Hill. I offered them a ride and we all piled into my Mustang convertible.

As we reached the main road, where the press corps was being corralled in a press area by the State Police, Senator Kennedy asked me to put down the top so he could chat with the reporters. I can only imagine the media's reaction as they saw me, the AP stringer, driving up in my convertible with the Kennedys. After several minutes of conversation with the press, we pulled away and headed to Garnet Hill. "What can we do for Ed?" Ethel asked her husband.

They decided to invite me to breakfast at the lodge for an exclusive photo shoot with their family. It was a coup for any photographer and an unheard-of opportunity for a stringer. Of course, I had to be sure that Eddie Adams got to come along, too. I didn't relish the thought of informing Eddie, who was not happy about the day's events and felt I led him on a long hike to nowhere and wasted his time while UPI got better access.

As we were reviewing and editing our photos from the day, it was obvious who was the pro and who the stringer. Eddie had a prize-winning picture of the Kennedys shooting whitewater rapids in the raft. I had an ordinary portrait with Senator Kennedy and nieces Caroline and Courtney, along with other family members. I should have been elated that it was my rather routine family portrait and not Eddie's dramatic action shot that ended up gracing the front page

of the Sunday New York Times and many other newspapers, including the Albany Times Union. Instead, I had to take heat from Eddie. He was mad at me, and rightfully so.

The next morning, we spent about an hour photographing the Kennedys at Garnet Hill Lodge: shots of the kids clambering in and out of pup tents, playing touch football and other activities with the photogenic family. Eddie selected five pictures to move on the AP wire and send to newspapers around the country. Only one photo of the five was mine.

Wouldn't you know it? My Kennedy family portrait photo was chosen by the AP as the Photo of the Week from among the pictures submitted by their dozens of famous photographers from around the world. My photo was honored further when it was exhibited at Rockefeller Center. If you looked closely during the exhibit, my photo appeared with an Eddie Adams photo credit under it. The stringer never got his due.

Believe me, I've never said a word about it. Until now.

***

Chapter 5:
Breaking & Entering Prague

Ed counts on Maureen for many things, including breaking and entering in Prague during an official visit with the International Olympic Committee. Maureen's second-floor job may have attracted the interest of this KGB agent, obvious in his surveillance.

We were used to going to extremes for our clients, but break-ing-and-entering was a first for us at Prague University during an official visit with the International Olympic Committee. We needed to re-type a contract under the Lake Placid Olympic Organizing Committee's jurisdiction that was critical to our work. But this was the Communist era and typewriters and fax machines were in short supply in Prague. The IOC Secretariat's press center, set up at Prague University, was our only hope. But it was locked up tight this weekend. We had no other option. We decided to make our break-in during the wee hours after midnight, under the cloak of darkness.

We had accomplices, notably our good friends from Lake Placid, Art Devlin, the famed ski jumper and ABC Sports Commentator; and attorney Norm Hess, the lawyer for the Lake Placid Olympic Organizing Attorney; as well as members of the IOC marketing committee. While other marketing committee members were illegally exchanging money on the black market, we cased the joint and spied an open window on the second floor of the building, which was about 12 feet off the ground. We didn't bring a ladder or any burglary tools. But we wouldn't be denied when our professional lives depended on reaching a typewriter, phone and fax machine. We chose to ignore the stern warning from the U.S. Ambassador in Prague, who told us that if we got into any kind of trouble, he would be powerless to get us out of any criminal jam behind the Iron Curtain since Czechoslovakia was still under rigid Soviet control at that time. As an aside, it should be noted that our friend, New York State Senator Ronald Stafford, who represented Lake Placid, had made the trip with us and I rewrote history (and caused Senator Stafford's jaw to drop noticeably) when I introduced him to the Ambassador as "Governor Stafford." Always a quick study, Ron played along with my ruse and didn't flinch when he was addressed as "Governor Stafford" by the Embassy staff and by Soviet officials who greeted us during highly formalized diplomatic rituals.

It gave me great comfort to know that I was aided and abetted by other lawbreakers as I lined myself up under the open window at Prague University, along with a couple of accomplices. We crouched down, locked my fingers together into a foothold not unlike a stirrup on a horse's saddle and boosted up Maureen. You might ask why I wasn't the brave soul to commit the crime of breaking and entering and why I offered up my wife as the perpetrator. I could lie and say she considered herself a B&E specialist, a true second-story woman. Actually, she weighed a lot less than I did, plus she could type like a demon, and she was a better climber. And she's just

generally tougher and gutsier than me. Of course, when I put my weight behind it, as I did as we commenced with our Prague break-in, I was an excellent booster. And the deciding factor was that the open second-story window led to the women's bathroom. We may have been committing a crime, but I drew the line when it came to invading the sanctum sanctorum of the women's lavatory. A guy could get himself killed for that.

And so, we managed to lift Maureen high enough so that she could grab the window sill and hoist herself through the window. Since we didn't hear any screams of pain when she dropped onto the floor of the women's bathroom and there were no alarms or armed KGB men descending upon us, I realized that our plan had worked. A few moments later, Maureen emerged in the press room, turned on a light, opened a window and spoke in a low voice to us, her lookouts, down on the street. We were committing larceny by committee. Devlin, Hess and I were conferring on the ground and when Maureen popped her head out the window, we'd whisper the changes she needed to make to the contract, and she'd go back to the typewriter and type them up. This went on for at least fifteen minutes, but it seemed like hours. I was sweating over every minute of the job, since Czech Uzi-toting soldiers patrolled the main square no more than 100 yards away around the corner. I was sure they would shoot first with their rifles and ask questions later. The time seemed to crawl past, second by agonizing second, and I wondered if Maureen was typing "War and Peace" up there. By the third time that she popped her head out the open window, I hissed that we better wrap this up and hightail it out of there or we'd be caught and banished to some gulag to perform hard labor.

Of course, Devlin and Hess thought it was a bit of a lark and snickered as they saw me growing increasingly paranoid.

Finally, Maureen said she had finished typing the revised contract. She shut the window, turned off the lights in the press center, scrambled out the women's bathroom window and we all reversed the procedure and lifted her safely down to the ground. Maureen had finished her mission impossible and she and her accomplices slipped silently down the darkened street, the soldiers still oblivious to the fact that the great Prague caper had just been pulled off under their noses.

We thought we had committed the perfect crime, but it was clear that the Communist authorities had put a tail on us. As the only woman among the delegation, Maureen was assigned her very own KGB agent, who never let her out of his sight. It was real cloak-and-dagger stuff, but it had its humorous moments. As this picture attests, the KGB agent who was following Maureen as she stopped to admire the fresh-cut flowers in a street cart was comical because he was so blatantly obvious. The fellow looked like he came out of central casting, with his spy trench coat and folded newspaper to make it look like he wasn't staring at Maureen. We were never afraid of this KGB man, who never spoke to us. After a few days of being followed everywhere, we got used to his presence and we were fortunate that we never got collared for breaking into Prague University.

Suspicious cars like this one also tailed Maureen during our Prague visit with the IOC.

Chapter 6:

Do you believe in Miracles?

The USA hockey team's "Miracle on Ice" upset victory over the Soviet powerhouse was a defining moment of the XIII Olympic Winter Games in Lake Placid. Behind the scenes, Ed clashed with coach Herb Brooks, who tried to keep his players from the press while Ed's job was to make the team more readily available to the media.

The U.S. Olympic hockey team's victory over the supposedly unbeatable Russians was not the only miracle on ice at Lake Placid. It was miraculous that USA hockey coach Herb Brooks and I didn't drop our gloves and square off in a fight at center ice. He was a really intense guy, to put it mildly, and our jobs and responsibilities naturally put us in conflict. His job was to keep the media away from his players so that they wouldn't be distracted and could remain focused, thus playing their best on the ice when it was game time. My job was to get the media as much access

as possible to his players, since they became the biggest story on the planet after defying all expectations and defeating the heavily favored Russians.

Brooks' team earned the nickname among the press office staff as "Peck's Bad Boys," because they were often difficult to control and their behavior with the media could be wild and crazy. They could be crude and got a kick out of trying to get a rise out of the reporters with their antics. But as soon as Coach Brooks walked into the press center, the big, bad hockey players turned into a bunch of choir boys. I'd never seen such a transformation. It was another

miracle on ice. It was obvious that they were afraid of upsetting Brooks and drawing the coach's wrath.

There was never any outright animosity between us, but believe me, I contemplated a few things against Coach Brooks that would have landed me in the penalty box. But we were two pros who held our tongues and manned up when it came to working together despite our competing interests.

Chapter 7:
Oh, Lord

Lord Killanin, President of the International Olympic Committee and a member of Irish royalty, got along tolerably well with Ed, but the old baron got googly-eyed around Maureen and flirted openly with her.

Maureen was responsible for building the great relationship we developed with the President of the International Olympic Committee, Lord Killanin. This helped us immeasurably in our jobs. From the earliest stages of planning for the Lake Placid Winter Games, he took a shine to Maureen and asked her to accompany him on venue tours. Luckily, I'm not the jealous type, even if he had an impressive royal title from Ireland The Third Baron of Galway. Besides, Lord Killanin was old enough to be Maureen's father. He preferred to dine at the private Lake Placid Club and occasionally invited Maureen or both of us to join him. One night, after a late dinner at the Lake Placid Club, I had to enlist the help of our friend, Geoff Miller, who was on loan from the Associated Press's London bureau and was covering the Olympics. Following a late-night round of cocktails, Lord Killanin needed help negotiating the spiral staircase down from the special perch where we had been drinking. Geoff and I helped carry the Irish royal and President of the IOC down the twisting, curving staircase and into the lobby. We managed to get him into the club lobby, where he fell to the floor and intoned these words in his lovely Irish lilt: "There are a lot of great things about the Olympics," he said, pausing for dramatic effect, "but one of the greatest is one can get pissed once in a while."

We managed to carry him to his hotel room, but the young man at the front desk would not give us the key to the Lord's room because he had been instructed not to because of security concerns surrounding the IOC President. We pleaded with the desk clerk, but he would not hand over the key, even when I showed him my all-access Olympics credentials and we explained the situation. When he was distracted for a moment, I reached behind the desk, grabbed Lord Killanin's room key off a hook and told the guy behind the desk we were taking him to his room. He said he was calling the State Police. Maureen, Geoff and I carried him to the elevator and never looked back. We managed to roll Lord Killanin into bed and were preparing to leave when two State Police troopers barged into the room with their guns drawn. We knew better than to try to make a joke or to say anything, so we put our hands up and kept our mouths shut. They questioned us for a few minutes, apologized to us and thanked us for getting the IOC President back safely. We closed the hotel room door quietly behind us and left Lord Killanin sleeping soundly in his king-sized bed.

***

Chapter 8:
Working with 'The Donald'

Long before he became famous for saying "You're fired!" on his hit TV show, The Apprentice, Donald Trump said "You're hired!" to our firm. For three years, we did P.R. and marketing for his cycling race, The Tour de Trump, which brought excitement and world-class road racers including three-time Tour de France winner Greg LeMond to Albany and other cities across the United States. The sprint through downtown Albany drew an international field and huge crowds of cycling fans. Maureen and I went on the road to handle press arrangements and promotion in each city, which meant we spent a lot of time with Mr. Trump, better known as The Donald. We discovered that he is a dynamic businessman and a true original as an entrepreneur. But Maureen, in her own inimitable fashion, quickly summed up the essence of The Donald: he drives a hard bargain. She felt we were underpaid for the account and she was probably right. But our Trump connection paid unexpected dividends by offering us an up-close and personal look at a hard-driving developer people either love or hate -- since it's impossible to be lukewarm about The Donald. I enjoyed hearing him talk about his Dad and the real estate deals they made in New York City.

We found out he can be generous, in his own way. After our three-year contract for The Tour de Trump concluded, he invited us to Atlantic City as his guest and our comped hotel suite was vintage Trump: a vast and tacky round bed, mirrored ceilings and over-the-top furnishings. Nobody would ever accuse The Donald of being taste-

When he was still Donald Trump and not yet "The Donald" and a reality TV star, he hired Ed Lewi Associates to handle marketing and media relations of his Tour de Trump bicycle road race that stopped in Albany. Trump also put the moves on Maureen during a private tour of his luxury yacht, to which Ed was not invited.

ful. He brought us aboard his yacht for cocktails one evening and it was jaw-dropping, of course. When he greeted us, he gave me a quick handshake and planted a big kiss – that lasted perhaps a moment too long, I felt – on the lips of Maureen and he immediately whisked her off for a private tour of his enormous vessel. I watched them disappear into a stateroom, slightly uncomfortable that The Donald had his right arm wrapped firmly around my wife's waist. I nursed a drink and waited...and waited. Finally, the two of them emerged from below deck. Maureen was giggling and grinning at something Trump had just told her. I noticed his arm was still firmly enveloping Maureen's shapely figure. That 15-minute tour, which included a one-on-one look at the master bedroom and other private areas of the yacht, apparently worked its magic. Maureen experienced a truly Trumpesque transformation because her grousing about the low-ball retainer he had negotiated for our work suddenly turned into effusive praise about what a great account and brilliant businessman Trump was. Maureen has never told me exactly what went on between the two of them on that private tour. Perhaps he let down his hair, or whatever one calls that stuff on his head. What's certain is that Maureen has always been Trump-struck after our evening aboard his yacht.

***

Chapter 9:
Oh, Deer!

Ed's use of animals to generate publicity for special promotions sometimes went awry. Two of Santa's reindeer got loose on a highway in Bear Mountain State Park during a charity toy gathering event and tied up traffic before State Police troopers and a handler from Santa's Workshop caught the runaway reindeer.

I used a lot of puns and wordplays in my career and staged unusual events, often involving animals, as a way to get media attention. So it was a natural extension of my interests when I decided to combine my off-beat sense of humor with a creative way to garner some press for a program to help kids at Christmas that I was helping to promote.

The set-up seemed innocent enough. I've always wanted to pose a deer at a Deer Crossing road sign, since I have driven hundreds of thousands of miles across this state and I have never seen a deer actually crossing near one of those signs. I figured it might be a literacy problem, since I don't think that deer can read and they didn't know they were supposed to cross at the signs put up for their benefit. In order to pull off the gag, I asked a client of mine, Bob Reiss, the owner of Santa's Workshop in the Adirondacks, if he could have his animal handler bring one reindeer to an area near a Deer Crossing sign where State Park Police had given me permission to set up. I guess Bob was trying to be helpful, because instead of one reindeer being led out of the truck, four reindeer emerged. My jaw dropped and that's when the action started.

It was a cold mid-December afternoon, two weeks before Christmas, and I was helping to promote "Operation Toy Lift," which was accepting donations for children at the Bear Mountain State Park, two hours south of Albany. Santa made an appearance and I had originally planned to have a single reindeer for posed still shots for the media who came to cover the event. The Deer Crossing sign in the background would be a bonus. Instead, the press got an action photo and live footage involving two reindeer who broke away from the handler and bolted down the highway. You might even call it a media circus, minus the ringmaster and big top.

When the two reindeer broke free and began bolting down the highway, Santa tried to spring into action by whipping off his red suit and attempting to lasso the runaway reindeer with a piece of rope. He chased after the animals, trying to make it seem like all part of the act by shouting "Ho! Ho! Ho!" But it was no go. In a matter of moments, the other two had gotten loose and now all four of the big, antlered beasts were roaming free and were beginning to snarl traffic as rubberneckers strained to get a look at this bizarre Christmas scene. The Park Police sent out a call for backup and both the New York State Police and the New Jersey State Police responded to the all-point bulletin that four of Santa's reindeer were on the loose. The troopers, fearing a roadway catastrophe of Rudolphian proportions, shut down both the northbound and southbound lanes of the Palisades Parkway for a 30-mile stretch. The last time something like that had happened was in 1969, when throngs of hippies arriving at Woodstock shut down the Thruway.

My simple idea of a photo op for a small group of local media in front of a Deer Crossing sign had morphed into something else entirely: TV news helicopters circling overhead, all the New York City newspapers had dispatched reporters and the national media and AP and UPI started picking up the story. "Operation Toy Lift" never expected this kind of lift. Yet we still had the unresolved matter of trying to catch four reindeer. They continued to elude the handler and even members of the media who tried to coax Santa's helpers back into their halters and into the truck. This crazy scene went on for more than two hours. I was told to get into the Park Police squad car – luckily, they didn't handcuff me and charge me with reindeer obstruction – we drove up and down the closed-off portion of the highway until we spotted one of the runaways. The cop pulled his service revolver. Instead of "Ho, Ho, Ho!" I shouted, "Whoa, Whoa, Whoa!"

"Hey, you can't shoot one of Santa's reindeer. That's just not right. Especially right before Christmas," I said.

"I'm not going to shoot one of Santa's reindeer. I'm going to shoot you," he said, turning the handgun on me. I noticed he wasn't smiling and my collar suddenly got a lot tighter and my throat turned dry.

Santa's runaway reindeer led the front pages and evening newscasts across the state and got a lot of play nationally. It helped generate record donations to "Operation Toy Lift." No reindeer were harmed in the making of the promotion. The handler finally caught one of the reindeer, which was just the ticket because the three other reindeer followed the leader and all four were safely returned to the truck, the highway re-opened and the media rushed off to file their stories. I wasn't sure whether to laugh or cry.

My buddy Bob Reiss at Santa's Workshop in Wilmington told me that the crazy day brought him to an executive decision: Never again would he loan me even a single reindeer. Not at Christmas, not ever.

Chapter 10:
The Tops

For the topping-off ceremony of the Marriott hotel on Wolf Road in Colonie, Ed came up with the concept of the "world's largest top hat." It was such a media sensation that the hotel chain incorporated the idea into it national marketing as "Marriott: The Tops."

I've always liked presenting a one-of-a-kind event and pulling off a media promotion that nobody else dreamed of or even thought possible. This proved to be a challenge with the Marriott Corporation, one of the national accounts we represented for several years. They are a world-class hotel chain that likes time-honored traditions such as throwing away the first key that is made to each room and folding the flag that is raised in front of each hotel in a specific fashion known as the Marriott style. When we were hired to handle media relations for a new Marriott hotel being built on Wolf Road in Colonie, I wanted to do something out of the ordinary. The typical Marriott tradition was to hold the same sort of a "topping-off" ceremony as the hotel neared completion, which included putting a pine tree on top of the highest steel girder as a sign of good luck. This was the same thing developers did for every other major building. I wanted our ceremony to be different, especially after I was told that the chain's CEO, Bill Marriott, would be coming to Colonie for the event.

Instead of a small pine tree, I came up with the concept for "The World's Largest Top Hat" for the topping-off ceremony of the world's largest hotel chain. There was only one problem. I didn't have a top hat. Of course, that never stopped me. I brought up the idea to the general manager of the Wolf Road hotel. He suggested that I go to the bar, enjoy a few cocktails on the house and lay the idea to rest. He told me there was no budget to build such a prop anyway, so just forget about it. I've been called stubborn on many occasions and this was one of them. I wouldn't let it go.

I went to my barber shop and talked to my barber, whose son was an ac-complished carpenter. Instead of asking my stylist to create a hairpiece to cover my bald head, I asked him to see if his son would be interested in building "The World's Largest Top Hat." He didn't laugh. He had heard some of my out-of-the-box ideas before. I met with his son and we sketched out my concept. He did some calculations and quoted me a price of $1,500 for all materials, rental of a flatbed truck and a crane. I was elated. This was definitely doable, I thought. The problem was that the client thought it was too much money and they put me off for awhile since they didn't want to spend the cash. Eventually, I wore them down and they green-lighted the idea.

Bill Marriott arrived to see the giant black top hat dangling over the nearly-completed hotel on a crane, along with a full contingent of media who came to cover the event. "The World's Largest Top Hat" could be seen for miles around and it was such a unique thing that it was included in "Ripley's Believe It Or Not." It also became a Marriott tradition and "The World's Largest Top Hat" was replicated and became part of each hotel's topping-off ceremony. It was even the basis for the hotel's tag line: "Marriott: The Tops." The top hat that my son's barber built had a recurring role. It was sold for $3,000 to a Marriott in Massachusetts. The most expensive top hat I learned about was one constructed to open the deluxe Marriott Marquis in the heart of Times Square at 45th Street and Broadway. I was told it cost $48,000 to build. Talk about inflation. My little idea had reached the big-time. I wished I had trademarked the idea. Although I never took credit for the "World's Largest Top Hat," it remains a Marriott tradition to the best of my knowledge and "Marriott: The Tops" had its genesis on Wolf Road in Colonie.

Chapter 11:
Banned in Boonville

Ed occasionally liked to go off script during promotional events as he did here by commandeering snowmobiles and roaring off with Goofy, Mickey Mouse, Snow White and Pluto. Ed's antics with the Disney characters the winter carnival were a crowd favorite and earned him a moniker: Banned in Boonville.

Given our long, snowy winters here in the Northeast, it made sense that we would represent snowmobile manufacturer Ski-Doo. Part of our job involved being on hand for snowmobile races, which were held on Sundays throughout the winter months, mostly in the Adirondacks. The biggest event of the year's racing season was the World Snowmobile Championships, which was scheduled to be held in the rural Oneida County village of Boon-ville, located in the North Country near Old Forge. It got a lot of snow, which made it an ideal location for the championships. The problem for us was that the Ski-Doo snowmobiles were experiencing a lot of technical difficulties and were literally falling apart on the track. Competitor Polaris was cleaning our clock, both on and off the track, in terms of press attention and coverage. The situation tweaked my competitive spirit. I couldn't do anything to fix the broken Ski-Doo machines, but I could remedy the other part.

We had a strong relationship with the Disney Corporation, since we had handled many special events for them across the Northeast. At the same time as the snowmobile races, the Disney characters were performing a revue called "Disney on Parade" in Syracuse, a two-hour drive from Boonville. I happened to know the show manager talked him into loaning to us for an afternoon four of the more popular Disney characters: Mickey and Minnie Mouse, Goofy and Pluto. My plan was to bring them to Boonville to lend a little excitement to the Ski-Doo operation and to draw added media interest and bring out more families with small kids, who didn't care about the snowmobiles but loved the Disney characters.

The Disney characters worked their magic and Ski-Doo was pleased with the dramatic turnaround. I talked Mickey and Minnie into driving snowmobiles, while Goofy and Pluto hammed it up as race officials waved checkered flags and entertained the crowds. It was a home run. Everyone was eating it up and in hindsight I should have stopped right there and quit while I was ahead. But I couldn't help myself when it came to one last bit of mischief.

Since Polaris was continuing to run laps around the Ski-Doo team and we weren't winning any heats, trophies or photos with Miss New York State, I decided we would stage our own Ski-Doo award event. I had the Disney characters grab the trophies, Miss New York State, and all the champagne on ice. We all loaded onto the back of a bunch of snowmobiles and took off. This time, the Ski-Doo machines didn't break and nobody could catch us. We were cracking up over our shenanigans as we roared away, but apparently the organizers and village officials on hand didn't see the humor in my impromptu gag. They were not amused. We got a lot of front-page photos out of it and plenty of coverage, but it also earned me an unexpected distinction: Banned in Boonville.

***

Chapter 12:
A Date with Maureen & a Lion

On one of their first dates, Ed convinced Maureen to pose with a playful lion at the International Amusement Convention.

I'm not sure what Maureen heard about me before we started dating, but I assume she knew that I had a reputation for bringing in animals as a way to promote events. But I'm sure nothing prepared her for her first adventure with me and my wild kingdom. The setting was the International Amusement Convention, a large trade show that I attended because of clients such as Storytown USA and other attractions with live animal acts. Maureen and I had begun dating and she agreed to join me at the convention. I knew several of the participants and ended up borrowing what I was told was an extremely mellow lion, which turned out to be playful and rather rambunctious. I was a fool for love and was trying to impress Maureen. I'm just lucky the lion didn't try to eat me for lunch.

Picture us in a large ballroom and I've got this 250-pound lion on a small leash. We quickly drew a crowd. We paused for a picture and Maureen was actually smiling as she kneeled down beside the lion. I was a bit nervous, but it worked out alright. Maureen got her first glimpse into my love of animals and was given fair warning about my unorthodox way of doing things. For me, it was the perfect fit: an exotic big cat and a sexy lady. I guess the combination worked. As I write this, Maureen and I have been married for 39 years…and counting

Chapter 13:
Marylou Whitney & Lew Swyer

Marylou Whitney is known as "The Queen of Saratoga" and has always been a good sport when Ed asked her to do something zany, such as riding an elephant. She teamed up with developer and philanthropist Lew Swyer, SPAC's Chairman of the Board, standing on firm ground, to help create the Saratoga Performing Arts Center, a crown jewel of "The Summer Place to Be."

We've had the opportunity to work with some extraordinary people during the many years we ran Ed Lewi Associates. Two of the most remarkable philanthropists, who did so much for Saratoga Springs and the Capital Region's cultural heritage, are Marylou Whitney and Lew Swyer. They were two of the primary movers and shakers behind the creation of the Saratoga Performing Arts Center, a jewel in the region's crown. I never had any trouble handling press for a Marylou event because she was up for anything that sounded like fun, she didn't mind being carefree and silly, and she never backed down from a challenge. I love the photo of Marylou riding on an elephant to open another season of SPAC, with Lew Swyer walking alongside her. He was a classy gentleman playing the straight man for the Queen of Saratoga's grand entrance on board a pachyderm, which I lined up through my circus connections. As you can see from the picture, Marylou was having a grand time and she loved the theatricality of the elephant entrance. It was classic Marylou, who asked one thing from me above all else: Never be dull or ordinary.

Chapter 14:

Friends for Life: Marylou & John

Ed and Maureen are proud to call Marylou Whitney and her husband, John Hendrickson, two of their dearest friends and a couple who are close enough to qualify as "family."

I've known Marylou Whitney for more than 40 years and she and her husband John have become good friends to Maureen and me. We've been part of her legendary parties for many years and have joined them on cruises and other vacations and have socialized with them on countless occasions. They're a fun couple and we never fail to have a good time together.

I'm lucky Marylou doesn't hold a grudge and that I didn't destroy our friendship even before it started, given our disastrous introduction. I met Marylou Whitney for the first time in the late-1970s for a media event at SPAC, whom I was representing. Marylou had donated a beautiful Steinway piano to the performing arts center and its debut performance was at a Philadelphia Orchestra concert led by Eugene Ormandy, with famed pianist Andre Watts as the soloist. The concert drew a huge audience and was a big hit until a crescendo a few minutes before the conclusion of the performance. Marylou's donated Steinway, billed as "the world's greatest piano," broke down and somehow I was left holding the bag — and the busted instrument.

It turned out the pedal board malfunctioned and a few pieces, which apparently hadn't been installed correctly, clunked loudly to the stage floor. The piano solo stopped immediately and the audience of more than 5,000 classical music fans began to laugh. Andre Watts got down on his knees under the Steinway and tried to fix it, while Ormandy stormed off the stage in a huff. There was more nervous laughter and stunned silence in the amphitheater and up on the lawn seats for people who had a view of the stage. This was bad. Really, really bad.

Marylou and Maureen, they like to giggle!

I happened to be standing just off-stage, in the wings, when Marylou, in her formal evening gown, stomped up to me in her high heels, grabbed me by the front of my shirt and said: "I don't know your name, but they tell me you are the P.R. person. So, what do I tell the audience?"

It all happened so quickly, I didn't have time to think or to devise a strategy. I just said she should tell the audience the truth, that mistakes happen and that she regrets the interruption to the performance but that she knows the Steinway people will make it right. It was my first encounter with Marylou and I immediately saw she was good on her feet and had a nice, light touch. She defused the tense situation with humor by asking a nurse backstage if we could get lots of bandages so that we could patch up the sick piano. Marylou helped direct the hubbub backstage as stagehands removed the busted Steinway and wheeled in a Baldwin piano replacement.

As it happened, Mr. Steinway was in the audience and he instructed his people not to let the press photograph the disabled piano. This would be bad for business. But I was in charge of P.R. and I had a line of members of the media demanding to see the piano, which was covered with a large white cloth like a patient in the intensive care unit. I decided to let the press take pictures and have a look at the Steinway, since I knew it would generate a tremendous amount of publicity for SPAC. I was working for SPAC, after all, not for Steinway. I slowly, dramatically pulled back the cloth to reveal the stricken grand piano. The video cameras and motor drives whirred and clicked. The disabled Steinway made it on the front page of The New York Times, as well as nearly all the local newspapers. The officials at SPAC loved the coverage. Marylou and I forged a friendship on the spot and she loves to tell that story when Maureen and I start sharing funny stories when we get together with she and John. I never heard from Mr. Steinway. I assume he wasn't amused.

Chapter 15:
Olympic Games Love Marylou

Although it was not publicized at the time, Marylou Whitney made a $100,000 charitable contribution to the 1980 Winter Games in Lake Placid, which alleviated serious financial troubles and helped make the Olympics a success.

Few people realized how serious the financial difficulties were that we faced in Lake Placid, from the transportation problems to simply paying our bills. The Olympic Committee, unbeknownst to the public, was having trouble making payroll in the months leading up to the 1980 Winter Games in Lake Placid. That's when an angel investor arrived in the form of Marylou Whitney. It so happened that Sonny Whitney gave Marylou a gift of $100,000 to buy herself some jewelry or do whatever she wanted to do with it. That was big money in 1980. Remarkably, Marylou decided she didn't want to spend it on herself and instead wanted to donate the money to the Lake Placid Games.

She called me up and said she could send a $100,000 check with her daughter, Heather, who was a volunteer at the time and who later worked with us as a staff member in the press operation. Marylou only had one question: To whom should she make out the check? I hesitated for a moment because it turned out that the Olympic Committee hadn't paid us yet and they were two years in arrears in paying the agreed-upon fee to Ed Lewi Associates. They owed us a lot of money and that check would have come in very handy for my family and our business. I didn't seriously consider that option and told her to make the check out to the XIII Olympic Winter Games.

The Olympic Committee was ecstatic when Heather handed off to me a rumpled, tattered check for $100,000 that she had stuffed into her pocket. It turned out to be the single largest donation ever made to the Games and it kept the operation solvent and helped them make payroll.

I carried the check to the controller's office and before I handed it over to him, I said: "If I were to give you a rather large check, do you think you could spare a few thousand dollars for my company since we have not been paid for two years?

"How big is the check, Ed?"

"It's 100K," I said.

There was a moment of silence. He cleared his throat and said, "Yes, we could spare a few bucks for you."

Nobody knew the Olympics savior that Marylou truly was. But she didn't end her support there. She played a leading role in the social scene in both Lake Placid and in the Olympic Games in Sarajevo. There was no budget in Sarajevo for hosting parties for the International Olympic Committee and they asked Marylou if she would like to weave some of the social magic she was known for in Lake Placid. As soon as Marylou signed on as host, they'd never seen anything like that in Sarajevo. She got her friend Kirk Douglas, the movie legend, to come to a party and we watched as Yugoslavian women basically tore at his clothes on the dance floor in a frenzy to own a piece of his celebrity. Maureen saw his distress, swooped in, grabbed Kirk Douglas as her partner, and danced him out the door and made a getaway from the overzealous fans.

Marylou invited us to join her and Kirk and her guests and we dined at the same Sarajevo restaurant for three straight nights. There weren't any other fine dining choices and they knew they had a captive audience. I noticed that the prices on the menu went up each night. On the fourth night, the place was shut down and the front door was padlocked. I later learned that the government had shut down the restaurant for price gouging.

It was in Sarajevo that I recall the one and only time Marylou became seriously angry at me.

She and her renowned interior designers Stephen Stempler and his partner John Cronin had brought suitcases filled with red, white and blue silk ribbons for decorating the party she hosted in the president's palace. Marylou has the ability to make a room look like a million dollars with the simplest of materials. Her initial plan was to include Maureen and me in the decorating task. I flatly refused. "I don't do bows, Marylou," I said. But as I left the ballroom, I shouted over my shoulder, "I'm off to set up 'Good Morning America' for tomorrow morning."

Maureen helped Marylou and her designers with the bows and ribbons. Marylou was peeved at me, but I held my ground. And I still have never made a ribbon party bow.

She had forgiven me by the time that I had the mayor of Los Angeles and other celebrities from his city crash one of her parties, without invitations. Marylou took it in good stride. She was always flexible, good-humored and could go with the flow, as I learned the first time I met her over a busted Steinway at SPAC. We've been friends ever since. And she never asked me to make a bow again.

***

Chapter 16:
Seriously Now, They're the Best

Marylou and John have done more to champion charitable causes across Saratoga Springs and at the Saratoga Race Course than anyone else. They are Spa treasures.

I can't stress enough the important part in our lives that Marylou and John have played. Marylou has been along for the ride with Maureen and me on more occasions and in more ways than we can count. She's definitely part of our inner circle and we deeply value her long and abiding friendship. Marylou and John are "family."

Marylou is at the heart of our four-decade relationship with the New York Racing Association. In our work with NYRA as a client, Marylou, and more recently, John, helped us tremendously with local and national press. While Maureen and I conscientiously contacted national media friends and associates in an effort to promote the human-interest side of thoroughbred racing and to entice casual fans to visit Saratoga, Marylou was our secret weapon in accomplishing this goal. We had a wide range of feature story ideas that we presented to our national media contacts during our work in marketing the track in the 1980s, 1990s and in the early 2000s.

As soon as an editor or producer came upon the name "Marylou Whitney" in our list of ideas, that often led to a story assignment. Marylou was fully committed to promoting Saratoga in every way possible. She did everything from squiring around the crew of NBC Nightly News for four full days and nights, to learning all that there was to know about Victorian architecture so that she could be a local expert for Robin Leach's show, "Lifestyles of the Rich and Famous." Marylou led the flamboyant TV host on a tour of the stately mansions on North Broadway that were rented by famous horse owners and trainers as their summer residences.

Whatever we asked of her, Marylou jumped in enthusiastically and was always a good sport about it. She also had great media savvy from her time making movies in Hollywood and her experience as a TV host and radio personality. She gave up countless hours of personal time to promote the places she loved: Saratoga and the race course. When John married Marylou, he joined her in those efforts to bring celebrities and famous people to Sara-toga and to entertain them like royalty during their visits – thereby generating a great deal of national publicity for Saratoga and for thoroughbred racing. As a result of their extraordinary efforts with the media and with their generous philanthropy for numerous local projects and causes, Marylou and John are in a class by themselves. We feel that they have done more than any other citizens to position Saratoga Race Course and Saratoga Springs as a world-class destination, the most successful thoroughbred track in North America and "The Summer Place to Be." The residents of Saratoga fully realize and appreciate the many significant ways that Marylou and John have contributed to the well-being of the city and the track. It is entirely appropriate that Marylou is known as the "Queen of Saratoga" and John has taken up his rightful place among Saratoga's royalty. They are an incomparable couple and they have left an indelible mark on the history of the city, the track and more.

We made the world's largest top hat for the Marriott chain and we tip it now for the grande dame of Saratoga, our dear friend, Marylou Whitney, and her wonderful husband, John.

***

Chapter 17:
Lilliputian Wedding

Ed came up with the idea for a Lilliputian wedding between two little people inside a tiny chapel in Storytown USA. After some minor modifications, the photographs and stories generated worldwide publicity for Ed's client, Storytown owner Charley Wood.

Some of the most popular attractions at Storytown USA, the precursor to the Great Escape theme park in Lake George, were brightly painted and cleverly decorated miniature houses that brought to life classic children's fairy tales, such as The Old Woman and the Shoe, Rumplestiltskin, Hansel and Gretel, Little Red Riding Hood and many more. These magical little buildings appealed to both grown-ups and children with their whimsical designs. I was looking for a way to promote Storytown with an unusual event that would get the media's attention. I played around with different notions in my head and then I struck upon the idea of a Lilliputian wedding. Lilliputians are very small people. They're not dwarfs or midgets. They're just very little people who take their name from Lilliput, an imaginary country of diminutive people as tiny as 6 inches tall in the novel "Gulliver's Travels" by Jonathan Swift. We had a few Lilliputians employed at Storytown in the summer novelty shows and two of them were engaged and planning to get married. I simply gave them the option of getting married on TV, in front of videographers and press photographers. They liked the idea. It had never been done before and it would be a historic event. I started making arrangements.

But there was a hitch, as often happens when I start to think outside the box. There is a tiny chapel among the miniature buildings in Storytown. It measures perhaps 6-feet high by 6-feet wide and is a scale model of a classic white clapboard New England church. I thought it would be the perfect place for a Lilliputian couple to wed. The problem was that the chapel had not been consecrated and thus was not officially sanctioned to hold a Roman Catholic matrimonial ceremony. I finally contacted the proper diocesan authorities, had the chapel consecrated and cleared that hurdle. It was full speed ahead, until my idea came to a screeching halt because the bride was so tiny – considerably shorter than 4 feet – that a nurse could not find a vein in her stick-thin arms from which to draw blood for a blood test in order to get a marriage license. After an hour or more of trying to find a vein, the nurse was successful.

Another large problem – the chapel was so tiny that it could only hold the Lilliputian couple and a Catholic priest who agreed to marry them. There was no room for the media or guests. We removed the stained glass windows so that the photographers could take pictures through the openings.

All the hassles were worthwhile, it turned out, since the Lilliputian wedding was a big hit with everyone and my client, Charley Wood, the owner of Storytown USA, was thrilled. Photos of Ruthie and her husband as they exited the chapel, showered with rice, appeared on TV stations and in newspapers across the country and photo spreads ran in major tabloids and magazines, including Life magazine. My favorite part of the event was seeing the joy on the faces of the tiny members of the marching band, including Ruthie, the smallest of the group, who carried a bass drum that was twice as big as she was. She pounded the drum with a steady beat and a big heart.

***

Chapter 18:

"Welcome World. We're Ready."

This banner boldly proclaims the completion of a frenetic construction schedule at the venues in Lake Placid for the Olympic Winter Games. The slogan, which Ed helped coin, set a tone of confidence and silenced critics.

Having secured the public relations contract from the Olympic Organizing Committee to be in charge of all the P.R. and media for the 1980 Winter Olympics in Lake Placid, Maureen and I set to work at building an organization and a network of friends and professional colleagues.

I made an early ally in Ray Lopez, project manager for Gilbane Inc., the construction manager for the Olympic complex. Ray was taking a lot of heat from environmentalists and naysayers who took any opportunity to criticize the building process in the years and months before the Olympic torch was lighted and the Games began. We decided to strike back against our critics and I came up with a bold and audacious slogan to underscore our public confidence – although, truth be told, in private we were all somewhat terrified at various points during the advance work, given the magnitude of the project. As an example of our chutzpah, even as the hockey arena and other major buildings were still under construction, Ray and I came up with a slogan to silence our critics: "Welcome World. We're Ready." We had those words emblazoned on large banners that we placed throughout the Olympic complex-in-progress and we hoped the optimism would begin to catch on and perhaps drown out the pessimists. In a way, I think the signs helped convince us that we were ready, although in reality we had a long way to go at that point to get ready for the Lake Placid Games.

Chapter 19:
It was not a Great Escape

"The Great Manzini" was a Houdini-styled water escape act that Charley Wood hired to promote his Gaslight Village on Lake George. But the not-so-great escape became a laughing-stock with its cheesy fakery, but the photos were published worldwide and brought Charley more publicity than he ever imagined.

There were no limits when it came to what I would do to drum up some good press for my mentor and earliest client, Charley Wood, in advance of the summer season opening of his Lake George attraction, Gaslight Village. Charley had hired a Houdini-type escape artist named Manzini as an act for the park. Manzini approached me about a media event, featuring him being submerged in the lake and escaping after a long, dramatic period underwater. I had never seen him in action, but his talents were highly recommended by

Charley. I planned this photo op stunt for the southern basin of the lake, with Gaslight Village in the picturesque backdrop. In addition to his escape artist act, I later learned that Manzini worked as an Elvis impersonator, as well as a magician and illusionist, fire eater and rock 'n' roll performer. Perhaps I should have been wary of his versatility. I also later discovered that he ran a peep show on 42nd Street in New York, but he worked cheap and Charley liked that aspect as much as I did. Practically every newspaper, TV and radio station within 150 miles sent a reporter and photographer.

I milked the build-up. I escorted a flotilla of boats out into the lake and when we reached the predetermined spot, we cut our motors and the photographers recorded Manzini as he stepped with great ceremony into his clear Plexiglass box. He was handcuffed and bound up in a strait jacket crisscrossed by chains, with several padlocks ensuring his imprisonment. The plan was for the clear box slowly to sink out of view, until it reached the bottom in the 20-foot deep bay and then Manzini, who was holding his breath, would work his Houdini-styled magic and escape. That was how we worked it out on paper.

But there was a problem with the design of the box and the logistics of his illusion. As more than a dozen still camera shutters clicked and numerous film cameras whirred, the self-proclaimed "Guinness World Champion Escapologist," remained bobbing on the surface of the lake and he was in plain view as he easily pulled apart the phony locks and clambered out a visible trap door in the box.

The assembled crowd witnessed this as clearly as I did. I felt the blood drain from my face. At that moment, I wanted to sink to the bottom of the lake.

Joe Paeglow, a United Press International photographer and a buddy of mine, laughed so hard and so hysterically that I thought he was going to fall out of his boat and become the victim of an accidental drowning. Immediately, the whole stunt was exposed as a sham, Manzini was seen as a fraud and the press had a field day mocking the big promo event I had staged. It's strange how things turned out.

We were front-page news all over the state. I wouldn't have gotten that much press if Manzini had drowned in the lake. I took a lot of ribbing, but I didn't take it personally and it didn't hurt Gaslight Village's business. Charley Wood shrugged the incident off, as well, and I continued to work for him for many years after the great Manzini tanked. Personally, I had developed a thick skin long before that Lake George fiasco. I was just trying to do my job, after all, but it was my bad luck that the escape artist had el cheapo equipment. I lived to promote another day, learned to roll with the punches and how to laugh at myself. Something positive had come out of the Manzini debacle after all: mailbags of newspaper clips from all over the country, and each one mentioned Gaslight Village.

***

Chapter 20:
Santa Arrives by Chopper

The show must go on at a special event and Ed was always ready to step in to rescue a project. When Santa Claus was a no-show, Ed donned the red suit and arrived in a chopper to the delight of dozens of young children who were waiting to sit on Santa's knee and share their Christmas gift wishes.

Growing up, my family celebrated both Christian and Jewish holidays, so I had no ecclesiastical issues with playing Santa. Besides, a hefty ad sales commission from a double, full-page ad for the Times Union, where I was an ad salesman, was riding on my ability to portray a credible Saint Nick. The client bought the giant ad because I had come up with an unusual Santa arrival idea that had never been done in our area. The only problem was that the Santa that had been hired by the store chickened out of the helicopter gig at the airport. I volunteered for the helicopter portion, but we had agreed that we would change places at the store, and the other Santa would pick up his assignment for the remainder of the day. After emerging from the helicopter, I learned that he was a no-show.

Not wanting to disappoint small children, Santa Ed soldiered on. I grew into the role. I was born 100% ham, after all. I smiled and jiggled my big, padded belly and bellowed "Ho! Ho! Ho."

Playing Santa was an education, even for this father of two. In the end, Santa Ed spent four hours listening to a long line of dozens of kids whose parents brought them up to sit on Santa's knee and tell him what they wanted for Christmas. The big, scary stranger in the red suit had a deleterious effect on the bladder control of small, frightened children. By the time I finished my four-hour marathon, I had a pee stain on the knees of the red suit rental as large as Lake George. As it turned out, I got my hefty ad commission and scored points with my boss and I earned every bit of it. I never played Santa the rest of my life.

***

Celebrities

Ed and Maureen worked and socialized with many celebrities. Here is a sampling from their extensive collection of photos.

Lou Jacob was one of the most famous clowns who ever lived.

Bob Hope

Two O'Connors (no relation) - Donald and Maureen, whose maiden name was O'Connor.

Principal dancer Edward Villella was a popular figure who was always willing to promote the ballet. He was an outstanding athlete including being a professional baseball player. After his career as a dancer, he founded the Miami City Ballet.

Beverly Sills: Warm, wonderful and talented.

The very funny Victor Borge was spectacular at the sold - out children's concert at SPAC, which I sold to McDonald's. It was entitled "McMusic." He is pictured here with Ronald McDonald.

Glen Campbell

The Carpenters

Robin Leach, host of "Lifestyles of the Rich and Famous" featured Marylou and Saratoga. His show was one of the many national television features that we did to position Saratoga as the Summer Place to Be.

Former Miss America and Hollywood celebrity Mary Ann Mobley was one of the many celebrities Marylou Whitney invited to Saratoga during the years we were all trying to position Saratoga as an important happening of national significance.

Governor Hugh Carey was in office during the Olympics in Lake Placid in 1980. His marriage to Evangeline "Engie" Gouletas made big news in New York and beyond.

Skitch Henderson "Mr. Music"

Following Ron MacKenzie's death, Reverend Bernard Fell became President of the Lake Placid Olympic Organizing Committee. Ed affectionately dubbed him "The Rev."

Marylou, Ed and Liza Minelli: Marylou had known Liza as well as her mother Judy Garland, for many, year, and when Liza came to Saratoga for a concert at SPAC, Marylou invited her to the National Museum of Dance Gala that Marylou founded for the museum. Liza appeared several times at SPAC and she sat outside the green room and signed autographs until the last picture got autographed. She was very good with the public and posed for photos. She was sweet as could be. She said, "Ed, that's what it's all about."

Suzy Chaffee (Suzy Chap-Stick) photo, signed "To Ed, King of P.R., Love from the Queen of Snow." Suzy was in Lake Placid with Gordon of Sesame Street to be "King and Queen of Winter". She was at the Golden Arrow Motel while Maureen and the Lewi's "daughter" Ann Leslie Uzdavinis polished her speech at home. Suzy was expecting Ed to bring the speech but Ann Leslie offered to make the delivery. When Annie returned home she informed Ed, "Sorry, I should have let you go - Suzy opened the door and accepted the speech, stark naked." Annie stole Ed's fun for the day. Ann Leslie lived with the Lewi's following the death of her parents when she was 18 years old. She became a full - fledged part of the Lewi family, as did her Old English sheep dog, Jasper. Annie worked for ABC during the Olympics, but true to her promise to Ed and Maureen she returned to college to get her degree. She is a successful producer today, living in Sausalito and Hollywood, CA.

Ed and Maureen with Mr. and Mrs. Robert Mondavi at their winery in Napa Valley. The Mondavis were gracious, engaging and generous hosts with a myriad of fascinating stories about their growth to fame.

Paul Newman getting ready to present a bouquet of flowers to Barry Schwartz (seated to Paul's left). Barry, co-founder of Calvin Klein, and his wife Sheryl, to this day, are among the largest contributors to the Double H Ranch. On the far right is Max Yurenda who has headed up the camp for critically ill children since its inception for then twenty-five years ago.

A former Olypmic bobsledder and skier Ron, McKenzie was President of the 1980 Winter Olympic Games in Lake Placid. He died before the Games, at a pre-Olympic event. Ron had a heart attack in the judge's tower at the ski jump and fell out of the tower. It was very dramatic. "I'm glad I didn't see it, Ron was a nice guy and well respected by sports leaders." Ed said.

This might be one of the only pictures that shows Charley Wood sitting down. He went from 5 a.m. until after midnight most days. He was Ed's mentor and a close, dear friend. Ed finally convinced him to go to Aruba and he loved it.

Sarah Palin and her husband Todd, were unable to go to the Kentucky Derby to see First Dude run so Marylou and John invited them to the Belmont Stakes. Since their limo driver got lost and there were women in the ladies room with cameras, Sarah was unable to change her clothes as she had planned to, but she and Todd were just as sweet as could be, and conversed on everything, except politics.

Ed confers with Merv Griffin at the Desmond Hotel in Colonie after he hired Ed Lewi Associates to promote and market the local radio stations he acquired.

Ed and Maureen chat with Ivana Trump, a guest of Marylou Whitney and John Hendrickson during the Kentucky Derby.

Publicity

The key to getting widespread publication of publicity photos was timing, of course, and extensive use of the wire services for broad distribution. It was also critical to tie in the photos with current news events or trends to make them timely. Ed understood that including children, animals and beautiful women in publicity photos also helped ensure that they'd generate interest.

Albany Mayor Erastus Corning 2nd shares an umbrella with Mickey Mouse in front of City Hall during Ed's promotion of the bicentennial parade held on Wolf Road in Colonie in 1976.

Rex Billings manager of Storytown USA reads the "Nixon Winner" headline to democratic donkey who is obviously not pleased. This was a national wire shot that went far and wide.

Sammy Davis Jr. being carried into Charley Wood's Wax Museum near Gaslight Village, which housed wax likenesses of famous people.

Ed found two friendly dogs, put goggles on them and had Charley Wood's technicians help retrofit a dune buggy to create this whimsical Moon Rover for a publicity photo to tie in with Apollo 11's moon landing in 1969.

Ed staged a politically-themed newspaper promotion at Thruway Exit 24, with an "I'm For Carter" sign on an elephant in advance of the Democratic National Convention in New York City.

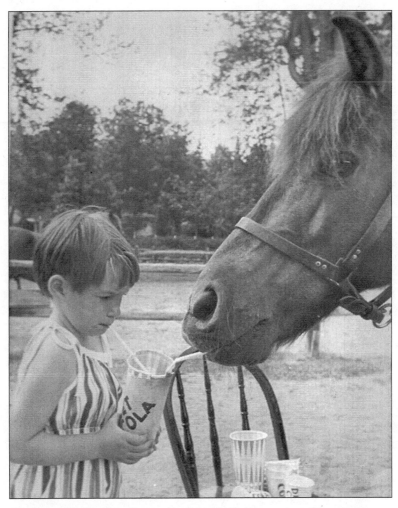

This photo featuring a cute 3-year-old girl drinking from a straw out of the same cup with a horse was sent out on the wires and published around the country. It was a big hit during Ed's promotion of a new beverage, Diet Cola, being sold at the Land of Make Believe Park in the Adirondacks, one of his clients.

Ed joins ballerinas with the New York City Ballet, along with a trotting horse and sulky at the Saratoga Harness Track to promote SPAC, horse racing and Saratoga as "The Summer Place To Be.

Ed was always willing to do his part for a publicity photo, especially if it involved beautiful young women in bikinis, such as these models in a promotional shoot for the Tiki Motor Inn in Lake George, owned by Ed's client Charley Wood.

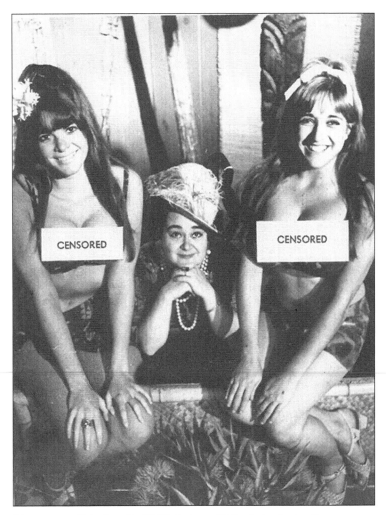

A humorous outtake from the Tiki Motor Inn publicity photo shoot, with a woman known as Hurricane Hattie in the middle and two models who went along with the visual gag while keeping their tops on.

Bears were an even bigger marketing draw than babes, Ed learned early on, and he hit it big with a bare-bottomed baby feeding a bear cub and his caption "bear essentials." The Great Escape promotional photo went on the wires and was published across the country.

Ed was a photographer who understood that timing is everything. He got this local cop on Route 73 near Lake Placid to oblige when Ed asked him to stop traffic and help the bear cubs cross the road. Ed's clients included 11 Adirondack amusement parks and attractions, two of which had bear acts. This publicity photo ran in newspapers all over the country. It was an extraordinary marketing coup for his clients.

Chapter 21:
Bicentennial Parade

World-renowned animal trainer Gunther Gabel Williams and the State Police saved the day for the parade.

efore I left newspaper work for good, I came up with one final major promotion for the Times Union in 1976. It was a real doozy, and turned out to be one of the highlights – or lowlights, depending on your perspective -- of my entire career at the paper. It was the bicentennial year and a lot of celebrations were being planned to mark the 200th anniversary of the founding of the United States in 1776. As the cornerstone for a huge 200th anniversary special section for the Times Union – a 180-page broadsheet, the largest ever produced by the paper — I developed a bicentennial parade in Colonie. For this patriotic celebration I chose Wolf Road, the Capital Region's fastest-growing commercial strip, at the busy intersection with Central Avenue. It turned out to be the largest parade ever held in Colonie. The only problem was that nobody was prepared for a bicentennial celebration that enormous.

I brought in two huge draws, the Ringling Brothers and Barnum & Bailey Circus and Disney on Parade. These attractions and more brought tens of thousands of spectators to the parade. People came from across the Northeast and arrived in motor homes and trailers and parked on the side roads and in parking lots along Wolf Road. It looked like a giant R/V Park. In the days leading up to the parade, the traffic at Central Avenue and Wolf Road became a nightmare, which infuriated the store owners at the two shopping malls on that corner, Colonie Center and Northway Mall. The parade was a bust for them because their parking lots were full of freeloading R/Vers and the traffic was so heavy that it turned away would-be shoppers. I was happy to report that the biggest winner was the Times Union.

Of course, that was the upside. I had my share of headaches and tense moments, such as trying to put a positive spin on the crime created by the parade, including a burglary and a rape. One of the narrowly averted catastrophes was when the Ringling Brothers' promoter decided to take out to dinner the night of the performance all the roustabouts, the laborers who set up the circus equipment and make sure things go off without a hitch. The promoter thought it was a nice way to thank the guys for their hard work, but he was cutting it close and didn't anticipate the massive traffic jams in every direction. With less than one hour to go before the start of the show, I did a check of the circus train and found that the roustabouts were not back from dinner yet. The show could not go on without them. I found Gunther Gebel-Williams, the superstar animal trainer for the circus, who slept in a trailer alongside his beloved tigers and elephants and didn't like to let the animals out of his sight. He was a good guy and we'd become friendly on previous visits of the circus to Albany. Gunther told me that the roustabouts were long overdue from dinner and that if they didn't arrive soon, given how much preparation was required, the circus participation would have to be delayed or canceled altogether. It would be my job to make that grim announcement to the tens of thousands of spectators who had been lined up six- or seven-deep for a couple hours already. I knew that announcement would go over like a lead balloon. I wracked my brain for a solution because the show, as you know, must go on.

As I walked from the circus train across the parking lot of the Northway Mall out to Central Avenue – a car was useless in that traffic jam – I passed the State Police command post. And the idea struck me. I stopped to explain my predicament to the State Police. Within minutes, the commander dispatched two State Police cruisers, with lights flashing and sirens blaring, with a description of the promoters' van and the location of the restaurant where he brought the roustabouts to dinner. Their goal was to locate the stranded van and to lead them back to the circus train with a full police escort. I had the utmost faith in the State Police. I didn't want to think of the alternative if they didn't succeed in their mission.

What the parade extravaganza taught me was how much people expect and how demanding they can be, even for a free show. As I was rushing around after dispatching the State Police, I also had to serve as a parking attendant of sorts. One of the parade officials was widening a lane in anticipation of the animal entourage that would soon pass through to Central Avenue from the Northway Mall parking lot, but he was blocked in by an elderly woman. I asked her nicely to please move her car. She refused. She was a grandmother who had brought her grandson to see the circus and she had secured her front-row parking spot several hours earlier and she was not going to move for anyone since they could watch the circus pass from close-range from the car.

The 1965 Christmas parade in downtown Schenectady that Ed helped organize drew an estimated 100,000 people. The police were not prepared for a crowd that large, nobody could move and it was a disaster.

"I promised my grandson he was going to see an elephant up-close and I'm not moving," she said.

I replied, "Ma'am, if you'll move your car, I promise you'll see an elephant closer than anyone."

She wasn't convinced, but I explained to her that I knew Gunther and that I could, indeed, produce a close encounter with an elephant for her grandson. She was dubious. But after some pleading, I finally persuaded her to move her car.

I was as good as my word because I went over to Gunther, who was getting his animals ready for the parade, and explained the situation. He smiled and said it would be no problem to comply with my request.

Less than five minutes later, the grandmother was startled by a visitor reaching through the open passenger window of her car. She felt the hot, moist air exhaled by an elephant's trunk as her grandson squealed with delight (or fear) and leaned in close from the back seat.

"Is that close enough, ma'am?" I asked. She was speechless.

In the end, the State Police managed to find and bring back the roustabouts in time. The "greatest show on earth" stepped off in the parade on time, and without a hitch. The circus and Disney on Parade were big hits and tens of thousands of spectators went home happy.

I don't know how I had done it, but I had managed to avoid disaster with the Colonie bicentennial parade. It was a high-water mark for the town, and Wolf Road would never see the likes of that extravaganza again.

There were two post-scripts to the parade. I punched the promoter in his (generously proportioned) stomach that night after the circus was broken down and the animals were returned to their special rail cars. And I had secured a future P.R. client in Ringling Brothers and Barnum & Bailey Circus. They said they liked how I handled a crisis. I didn't tell them I was making it up as I went along.

Chapter 22:
Man in the Mud

Josie Beckos Wood, Ed Lewi and Charley Wood, both long-time friends and business associates.

I had a secret weapon in successfully making the leap into a new career after leaving the Times Union and establishing a full-time, full-service P.R. firm: My wife Maureen encouraged me to break away from the newspaper, convinced me that I had what it took to run a business and she was an indispensable partner on every step of the journey. Of one thing I'm certain. Without Maureen, I never would have made it. Even with my wife's unwavering support, it felt like I was making a major transformation. I didn't feel much like my usual loose, joking self given how much I was rolling the dice. I had left a good, stable job with a pension and benefits for the uncertainty of a start-up company. I was 42 years old, with two kids to support. Since Maureen was joining me in Ed Lewi Associates, we were going all in with our new venture.

We started quite modestly. I set up a small office on Route 7 in Latham and scrambled to supplement the couple of clients I had been working with during my years of moonlighting while at the paper. Besides SPAC and my newly-landed Price Chopper account, the core of the new business was my first client, Storytown USA, Gaslight Village and the other local attractions in Lake George that were created and owned by Charley Wood. He was an entrepreneur ahead of his time and I dubbed him "the father of theme parks" in all of our publicity material. He opened Storytown in 1954, which was more than a year before Walt

Disney opened Disneyland across the country in California. Charley built Storytown, which was based on Mother Goose rhymes, in Queensbury on swampy land a few miles outside the village of Lake George that he and his wife, Margaret, purchased for $75,000. Charley did a lot of the construction and labor himself, mixing cement and pounding nails. He threw himself into the project and often worked so late that he only got three or four hours of sleep each night. Charley was a true original who favored loud sports coats and loved to make a grand, splashy entrance behind the wheel of Greta Garbo's 1933 custom Dusenberg, which he owned for many years. Charley died in 2004 at age 90 at his home in Glens Falls and I was honored to call him my friend, mentor and a client for more than 40 years. As the New York Times noted in its lengthy obituary, Charley lived

10 years after doctors ordered him to stop riding his own roller coasters. Charley was a consummate marketer and he also understood the American consumer very well. He knew that the post-war prosperity and rise of the automobile created a large demand for a new sort of roadside attraction for a nation where large families, big cars and taking to the road on family trips was a potent new trend. Storytown drew young children with horse-drawn pumpkins and an actress portraying Cinderella and a replica of Cinderella's castle, while their parents could enjoy the Old West theme of Ghost Town and the entertainment of dramatic shoot-outs using local actors. Charley also understood the importance of a critical mass of theme parks and attractions and in the Lake George area he developed an empire of properties: amusement parks, resorts, restaurants, hotels, a classic car

Charley Wood sitting at his desk

museum, a wax museum and more. He was a family entertainment pioneer way ahead of his time.

I learned so much from Charley about chasing dreams and how to start and run a business. He also taught me the necessity of a strong work ethic and how to make work seem like play. He truly loved running his theme parks and remained a kid at heart throughout his life. Over time, he became one of my best friends. Our relationship had a funny beginning. Since I was assigned to the Lake George region as my territory when I was selling ads at the Times Union, I made a trip to see Charley, who had never bothered to advertise in our paper. It was raining and turned Storytown to mud, but ever the intrepid salesman, I carried my umbrella and crawled under a building where Charley was working on one of the miniature fairy tale displays that made the park famous. I surprised Charley, who glared at me. "Who are you?" he asked.

"I'm from the Times Union and I'd like to talk you about advertising in our newspaper," I said.

"I just bought it," Charley said with his characteristic grin.

He shook his head at the sight of me, wet and bedraggled after tromping through the rain and mud to meet him face-to-face. "Your suit is all muddy," Charley told me. "Go clean up and I'll come see you."

I found a bathroom, wiped off the mud on my suit, shoes and briefcase with paper towels and sat down with Charley in his office. He was a decisive guy. Within five minutes, he said he'd take out a full-page ad, which cost several thousand dollars. We shook hands on the deal. An even deeper and lasting friendship was sealed at the same time.

From that day on, Charley had a nickname for me: Man in the Mud.

***

Chapter 23:
Scoring the Olympic Contract

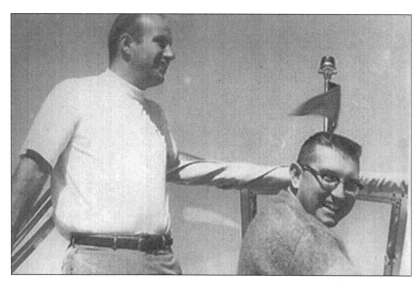

Ed was a David against Goliaths in his bid to win the P.R. contract for the 1980 Olympic Winter Games in Lake Placid. The small, upstart Ed Lewi Associates beat out the nation's P.R. giants, despite the fact that one of his "associates," photographer Joe Paeglow, seen here on a boat with Ed, fell asleep and snored through the initial meeting with Lake Placid officials.

A few months after I left the paper, early in 1977, I got wind from my North Country friends that the P.R. contract for the 1980 Winter Olympics was going to be put out for competitive bid. I had successfully represented Essex County and the Lake Placid Chamber of Commerce for several years, so I wanted to check out our competition for the contract. If we decided to throw our hat in the ring, we would be going up against the 16 largest, most prominent P.R. firms in the country. It was a plum project and all the big players from New York City to Chicago to Los Angeles wanted to win it. The early front-runner was Hill & Knowlton, one of the largest and most-respected P.R. firms, with numerous offices around the world. And there we were, Ed Lewi Associates, which was basically my wife and I plus two other employees. Talk about a David and Goliath battle. But I was never one to back down from a challenge. I decided we'd make a bid.

To make our odds even longer, I had the added liability of Joe Paeglow. I decided I'd bring along my old buddy, Paeglow, chief photographer for United Press International at its Albany bureau. I'd known him for years and we'd done a few side projects together – including several in the Lake Placid area.

What a mistake. That decision turned out to be almost a deal-breaker and nearly destroyed my Olympic dreams before they even got started. Paeglow was one of the unnamed "associates" of Ed Lewi Associates and he was familiar with Lake Placid because of his wire photo work, so Joe came along for the ride. I knew we were an extreme long shot for the contract, given the competition, but I figured we'd roll the dice. "What the hell," I said to Maureen. "We'll just go up and talk to them in Lake Placid." If I recall correctly, Maureen rolled her eyes and shrugged.

Our meeting with the P.R. firm selection committee was scheduled for a week night in the old 1932 hockey arena in Lake Placid. Paeglow had an early shift at UPI that day and I had to wait for him to finish his shift. We made the 2 1/2-hour drive and arrived in darkness. The committee consisted of Lake Placid civic leaders Jim Brooks, an attorney; Luke Patnode, the county promotion director, who had worked with me and was firmly on my side; and Dr. Robert Madden, a dentist and chair of the group. It turned out that two of them knew nothing about P.R. So, I at least had expertise and knowledge of the business on my side. On the other hand, I had Paeglow. The meeting had barely begun before Paeglow nodded off in his chair, his chin slumped into his chest and he began to snore. This did not endear me to the committee. We sat in a dark, dingy room and a single bare light bulb was suspended from the ceiling over the table where we sat. I felt like I was being interrogated on the witness stand at a criminal trial. "What would you do first?" Brooks the attorney asked, before continuing to press me in a belligerent way for details I couldn't provide.

Jim Brooks scowled and berated

me about Paeglow's slumber. I could hardly blame him for that. I was embarrassed by my sidekick, too. I bit my tongue and didn't say anything stupid. I wished I could have given it back to Brooks, who rubbed me the wrong way with a condescending attitude. Two of these three guys knew zip about P.R. and they essentially gave me a lecture on my craft and made me feel foolish for wasting their time. I was happy to cut the meeting short and drove home to Albany in silence. Paeglow snored some more. I was so mad at him my head was ready to explode, but I made it home safely without giving in to my urge to throttle him.

Brooks did not hide his disappointment over how poorly I had made my case for winning the P.R. contract for the 1980 Winter Olympics in Lake Placid. He made up his mind that I was the last person he'd pick for the assignment and he told his wife as much that night. When I got home to Maureen, she asked how it went. I described Paeglow's sleeping and the rest of the fiasco. "Besides, I'd never want to work with Jim Brooks. He's a real jerk," I said. "I know I didn't do well, but I might have made a better impression if Joe hadn't fallen asleep."

I tried to put the Olympics out of my mind and went back to grinding out the publicity and promotion for my clients, which included several seasonal attractions as well as the Lake Champlain Ferry Company and Fort Ticonderoga. A short time passed. And then, to my surprise, Dr. Madden, chair of the committee, contacted me and asked if I'd come up for a second meeting. I jumped at the chance. This time, I conveniently forgot to ask Joe Paeglow to join me. Nobody fell asleep and things went much better the second time around. I didn't even get a grilling by Brooks. I felt the tide turning and that I might still be in the running, after all.

I heard nothing for a few weeks, but started picking up a faint buzz that the big players, such as Hill & Knowlton, were asking for such a huge fee that they were pricing themselves out of the competition. They had massive payrolls, with expensive talent and large staffs, along

Jim Brooks and Ed became good friends and here they hammed it up at Divi in Aruba.

with huge overhead for premium office space in several cities. As a result, they had to price their work accordingly and their rates were off the chart. By comparison, with a tiny staff and little overhead, Ed Lewi Associates could at least out-compete the big dogs on price. I could hardly believe it when I was called and summoned to Lake Placid for a third meeting. This time, Joe Paeglow was a distant memory and I was wearing them down. It turned out that I had outlasted the major-league agencies and my local knowledge and affordable rates were trumping big egos and outsized reputations. In the interim, the trio of the public-relations committee met with the local Olympic organizing committee. I was told later that Dr. Madden summed up the discussion when he said, "We've got nobody we can afford, so we might as well try Lewi. At least we know him." It's been said that all's fair in hand grenades and horse shoes and I didn't mind that we landed the biggest gig of our lives essentially by default after Hill & Knowlton priced themselves out of contention.

I would have liked a ringing endorsement, but more important was the fact that Ed Lewi Associates had beaten out more than a dozen of the top P.R. firms in the country and we were now the official P.R. agency of the XIII Olympic Winter Games in Lake Placid in 1980. Looking back on it, they got us for a steal. We signed a six-month contract for $60,000, which was a small fortune to us with our fledgling business. And then I realized that Hill & Knowlton was likely asking for 10 to 20 times that sum and I should have tried to negotiate a better deal. Still, our company consisted of Maureen, myself and two other employees, so at least we didn't have to cut the check into too many pieces. The only problem was that we didn't get paid for nearly two years. Luckily, we had other paying clients, notably the Saratoga Performing Arts Center, or SPAC, and the Golub Corporation, which owned the Price Chopper supermarket chain – two major clients we'll discuss later. We were at least prepared for the Olympics challenge, since we had always been a lean and mean operation and we'd learned how to do a lot with very little. I even forgave Joe Paeglow and ended up hiring him from time to time to take pictures for us. He never fell asleep on the job. At least that I know of.

Chapter 24:
Olympics Ice Queen

Most of the staff involved behind the scenes at Lake Placid quaked in fear over Madame Berlieux, a powerful International Olympic Committee official from France dubbed "the ice queen" for her frosty personality. She was so warm and friendly to Ed, almost flirtatious, that friends teased him about his new French "girlfriend."

Nobody associated with the Olympics in Lake Placid, especially Maureen, could understand my unusually warm relationship with Madame Berlieux. She struck fear into the hearts of people and developed a reputation as a queen of mean. Yet she was so friendly to me that Maureen and others began teasing me about my "girlfriend," Madame Berlieux. She was a former Olympic swimmer from France and Executive Director of the International Olympic Committee. She was also tough as nails. She was a humorless old matron who seemed to relish her role as enforcer and security officer of the Olympic rings. She ran roughshod over local organizers as judge and jury. She was a pit bull in a skirt when it came to protecting the Olympic franchise. Essentially, from the moment that Lake Placid was designated as the Olympic site, she became the ice queen of protocol and did not mince words in warning the Lake Placid folks that they better not step out of line when it came to adhering to the rather archaic and complex play book of rules related to staging an Olympic Games. Within days of setting up shop in Lake Placid, she had no shortage of enemies. Many people openly despised her. Strangely, I was not one of the many Madame Berlieux haters. In fact, I kind of liked her. It was an acquired taste. Perhaps she felt no threat from me, since she was of Amazonian stature, with the broad and powerful shoulders of a champion swimmer and the height of a lumberjack. I'm sure she immediately understood that she could kick my ass without breaking a sweat if need be

The Olympics required a lot of international travel for both Ed and Maureen, but just prior to the Games Maureen won the coin toss. While Ed took all the trips that involved meeting with Madame Berlieux, Maureen traveled on Air Force One to Olympia and Athens , Greece, to pick up the flame and bring it to Washington D.C. for its trip through the original thirteen colonies on its torch run to Lake Placid.

and I never gave her provocation to test that theory. If anyone doubts that Madame Berlieux had a warm spot in her cold, cold heart for me, I can produce a picture of her kissing me on the cheek. I don't know what provoked it. It's a shocking image, since most of the photographs snapped of her at Olympics press conferences and other official events show a glowering, purse-lipped curmudgeon. I guess I have that effect on women, even the most rigid.

I always knew where I stood with Madame Berlieux as did everyone: It was her way or the highway. I never questioned her authority as the No. 2 person at the Lake Placid Olympics, behind only Lord Killanin. But even my warm, trusting relationship with Madame Berlieux had its limits. I learned as much in Prague, which is another story.

Chapter 25:
Getting Down to Skivvies

As the book's title suggests, babes were second only to bears in Ed's promotional arsenal. Here, he gets cozy with two beauties he hired to model long underwear in the style of 1932, left, and 1980, right, to promote the two years that Lake Placid hosted Olympic Winter Games.

I t's a truism every public relations man learns early on in his career. There's nothing like a beautiful woman to get attention, whether to promote a new product, to motivate photographers or to get the public to take notice. But I was never one to follow the crowd or to choose the obvious route. I decided that I could double the benefits by hiring two beautiful women. I found two gorgeous, curvaceous blonde models and decided to come up with an event to promote the Lake Placid Olympics during a pre-Olympic trip to Las Vegas.

I came up with the idea of creating for the media an unusual endorsement deal: The Official Underwear of the Olympic Winter Games. Since I had the two beautiful blondes to work with, the concept would be to highlight that Lake Placid was selected as the home of both the 1932 and the 1980 Olympics. Hence, the Official Underwear of the '32 and '80 Games with two sets of long johns: a pair of old-fashioned button-up flannel long johns and a more modern synthetic set of long underwear that skiers use. Somehow, I managed to get a Vegas motorcycle cop to go along with the gag and he ticketed the twin lovelies by writing them up for being improperly dressed in their underwear and causing traffic tie-ups because motorists kept slowing down and rubbernecking, thinking they were experiencing vision problems. It was a great little promo and had the intended effect by getting a lot of press and spreading the brand of the Lake Placid Olympics all the way cross-country from New York to Nevada.

Chapter 26:
Brooks & Team USA Hockey

The "Miracle on Ice" became one of the most memorable sports stories of the century, but another drama was going on backstage. Team USA hockey coach Herb Brooks and Ed argued over media access to the players and the two men were dubbed "fire and ice." Herb in foreground bites his nails as team does news conference. Ed is in the background, arms folded."

There were plenty of small dramas, little snafus and minor irritations going on behind the scenes all the time at Lake Placid and perhaps no more so than when it came to the celebrated USA hockey team and its "Miracle on Ice." For starters, although I made every effort not to let it show and certainly did not allow the media to catch wind of it, USA hockey coach Herb Brooks and I had a strained relationship at best. He was a really intense guy, to put it mildly, and our jobs and responsibilities naturally put us in conflict.

Throughout the pre-Games exhibition schedule and the Olympics itself, Herb and I butted heads and we played an increasingly aggressive cat-and-mouse game as he tried to block the press from interviewing and photographing his team and I did my utmost to make them available because it was the story everyone wanted to cover, all over the world.

I guess it was a classic love-hate relationship. We realized that we needed each other and we understood we were just doing our respective jobs, but that didn't mean we called a truce. The battle was joined anew each time I organized a press conference.

If a picture is worth a thousand words, this photo of Brooks is price-

One of the USA hockey players, John Harrington, is signing an autograph for Lewi's oldest son Joey.

less. Look at him gnawing on his knuckles with anger and frustration as his players talked to the media, while I stood on the other side of the photo, wearing a scowl and a no-nonsense attitude, making sure the press conference went smoothly.

***

Chapter 27:
Jimmy Lewi, Ski Bum

Ed's son, Jimmy, walking with his skis along Main Street in Lake Placid, was an 11-year-old ski bum in his element during the 1980 Olympic Winter Games. He blew off a request to give a tour to Amy Carter, the president's daughter, and instead went skiing on Whiteface Mountain alongside his idols, U.S. Olympic skiers Phil and Bill Mahre.

I remember getting a call from a White House staffer who asked me to find a good kid who was Amy Carter's age to lead her on a tour around Lake Placid. They were seeking a youthful diversion because the president's daughter would be under the care of a chaperone who was a stern, older woman. I immediately thought of my son, Jimmy, who was 11 years old. I thought it would be an amazing opportunity for him, a chance to squire around the president's daughter, the chance of a lifetime. "No way, dad," my son informed me when I gave him the breathless pitch. "Are you kidding me? You're crazy if you think I'm going to give up skiing with the world's best

skiers to take that brat around. I don't care if she is the president's daughter." We ended up finding a Lake Placid girl who was Amy Carter's age to fill in as a surrogate chaperone and everyone seemed pleased with the arrangement. Especially Jimmy.

To a ski bum like my son Jimmy, Amy Carter wasn't even in the same league in his mind compared to getting to ski with the likes of Phil Mahre and Bill Mahre on Whiteface Mountain. The Mahres were skiing royalty in Lake Placid. They were also a feel-good story of the 1980 Winter Games. After Phil's terrible fall and major injury at the Lake Placid World Championships in 1979, nobody expected that he could come back from his shattered ankle to regain his world-class ability and the great promise of his early career. Against all odds and the opinions of most skiing analysts, Phil Mahre not only came back from that injury, he managed to compete in all three Alpine skiing events at the Winter Games just 12 months later and did so with pins and screws holding together his damaged ankle.

Phil Mahre was my son's skiing hero and it wasn't hard to understand the admiration. Both Mahre brothers, and especially Phil, were excellent athletes, fierce competitors and stand-up guys. My son would never forget skiing alongside these legends and he was there to watch Phil compete in his improbable return to the Olympics, where he finished a distant 14th in the downhill and 10th place, another disappointment, in the giant slalom. Jimmy got to see Mahre's stunning first run in the slalom, when he took over first place by knocking the great Ingemar Stenmark out of the top spot. There was a buzz among the spectators, who were anticipating another classic Mahre performance. He challenged the big Swede and gave Stenmark a battle, but Mahre ended up with the silver medal and was cheered wildly for that extraordinary and brave performance given the catastrophic injuries he suffered just one year before in Lake Placid.

While Mahre was making headlines with his gutsy, inspiring skiing, we were helping negotiate the logistical nightmare of dealing with our VIP visitors, Vice President Mondale and Amy Carter. Mondale flew on Air Force Two, the luxury jet used to shuttle the veep to and from official ceremonies. He flew in and out of Plattsburgh Air Force Base, where Air Force Two was kept under tight security and ready to take off at a moment's notice in case Mondale was needed in Washington or elsewhere around the world. As President Carter's understudy, Mondale's official role at the Olympics was relegated to the opening ceremonies. It was a fairly easy 50-mile commute on lightly traveled back roads from Plattsburgh to Lake Placid for Mondale, given his Secret Service escort and convoy of State Police and local law enforcement vehicles with emergency lights flashing and sirens wailing. Mondale traveled to and from the Olympic venues with ease given his level of security and the short distance between Plattsburgh and Placid. He came and went from the Adirondacks without a glitch and returned in time to celebrate the Team USA's hockey victory over the Soviets.

***

Chapter 28:

Amy Carter & My Hockey Lesson

President Jimmy Carter sent Vice President Walter Mondale, greeting Ed and others, here, and the president's daughter, Amy, as goodwill ambassadors to Placid."
Ed managed to get Amy into the locker room to meet the USA hockey players.

T hings didn't get any easier for Amy Carter after the American hockey team beat the Russians. Her handlers wanted to milk the publicity with a photo-op and to use Amy as a stand-in for her father, President Jimmy Carter, who was dealing with the Iran hostage crisis and other problems that kept him tied down in Washington. They asked me to get Amy access to the players celebrating inside Team USA's locker room for a brief meet-and-greet following the pandemonium set off by their historic win against the Russians. Even before he heard the request, my old adversary Herb Brooks was ready to put the kibosh on the plan as soon as he saw me

walking toward him in a hallway leading to the locker room. He had to start planning for their next game, the gold medal game, against Finland, after all.

"Hey coach. We have a request from the White House to let Amy Carter in the locker room to meet the players and take a couple pictures," I said in my sweetest voice, trying to butter up the crusty Brooks.

"I don't let you in. I'm not going to let her in," the coach shot back at me.

He saw the displeasure register on my face and before I had a chance to come back with a clever response, he clapped me on the shoulder to indicate he understood the request was coming from a pay grade far above his own.

He was also savvy about how the media worked and a smiling picture with Amy Carter and his players couldn't help but assist his players' and his own post-Olympics prospects. He told me to give him a little time alone with his team and to bring the president's daughter to the locker room in 20 minutes and they'd accommodate the White House request. "It's pretty wild in there right now," he said. "Just let us clean up our act a bit before she comes in."

Brooks was as good as his word. The players were gracious gentlemen when I brought Amy into the locker room and they smiled for pictures with her and made small talk. Amy was just a kid and looked like a deer in the headlights. But she handled the situation pretty well, I'd have to say. She didn't cause any gaffes or ask silly questions. It helped that all the players had signed a hockey stick and gave it to Amy to present to her father, the President. She was excited to accept the gift, but obviously had never held a hockey stick before. She grasped it like a flag and waved it around in the locker room and over the heads of spectators as she sat watching the game against Finland, threatening to behead or at least severely injure players, her Secret Service detail and innocent bystanders. One of the Secret Service guys sidled over to me and whispered: "You gave her the stick. Now, you're in charge of her safety and the safety of other people." So, I pulled Amy aside and gave her a quick lesson in how to hold and handle a hockey stick. She wasn't an NHL prospect, but hopefully she wouldn't do any damage with the stick between here and delivering it to her dad at the White House. Luckily, Amy didn't skewer Vice President Walter Mondale when he came into the locker room to congratulate the players. He was very pleasant and had a nice rapport with people. He told the players that he and President Carter were going to invite them to a dinner at the White House. He said they could have whatever they wanted and he cracked everyone up by pretending to be a waiter and going around to the players and taking their dinner order. The emotion in the locker room was exuberant and the celebration was extraordinary.

***

Chapter 29:
Legends & Skating Heartbreak

Ed and Maureen became almost surrogate parents for several young Olympic athletes while handling the media frenzy in Lake Placid. They became particularly close to speed skater Eric Heiden, shown here, as well as Heiden's sister Beth, and figure skaters Scott Hamilton and Randy Gardner and Tai Babilonia.

During the Olympics, we got to work with Olympic speed skating legend Eric Heiden, who won an unprecedented five individual gold medals at Lake Placid while setting one world record and four Olympic marks. As press director of the Games, our office handled all athlete media appearances. Besides Eric, we handled press relations for his sister, Beth, also a speed skater, and all the figure skaters, including Scott Hamilton and Randy Gardner and Tai Babilonia.

But there is a backstory, as there often is with me. Before the Olympics, I took Beth Heiden to a liquor store.

She turned 18 – the legal drinking age for New York State at the time — on a day I was going to hold a press conference with her for a pre-Olympic event, a speed skating invitational a year before the Olympics. She said she would be happy to go to the press conference if I would take her to a liquor store first because she wanted a bottle of champagne to celebrate the milestone.

I took her to the only liquor store in Lake Placid on Main Street and hung out in the back of the store so that Beth, who wore Team USA warm-ups, could buy the bottle of bubbly herself. She was tiny and looked about 12 years old. Of course, the guy behind the counter asked her age and looked at me.

I nodded in the affirmative. She would soon have a lot to celebrate between the Heidens' heroics on ice.

Beth went on to win the bronze medal at the 1980 Olympic Winter Games. Her brother was so dominant that a Dutch newspaper called him the greatest skater ever. We had the greatest seat in the world to watch Eric make history because the speed skating oval was on the front lawn of the school, and we had our press operation set up in the library, with windows overlooking the speed skating track. All of our staff members could watch him race without getting up from our desks. Eric was a wonderful young man and the press loved him. He later traded his skates for surgical equipment and he became an orthopedic surgeon, and a damn good one, I'm told.

Eric delivered the Athletes' Oath at the opening ceremony of the 1980 Games, which he handled much better than his umpteenth interview about all his gold medals. He was at a press conference once and a reporter asked: "Well, Eric, what's it feel like to win your fifth gold medal?" He always wore a knit winter cap and he took it off, scratched his head, thought a moment and said, "Oh, sh--! I don't know what to say."

Dan Lynch, the managing editor at the Albany Times Union, who was overseeing the newspaper's Lake Placid coverage, told Heiden he couldn't use the colorful quote because it was a family newspaper and it might offend readers. I asked Eric to give the question another go and he did so, producing a family-appropriate response.

We worked hard to keep the press conferences worthy of a PG rating, but the hockey players could get a little wild and mouthy. But once their coach, Herb Brooks, walked into the room, they settled down and behaved like perfect gentlemen. Brooks had that effect on even the wildest players.

While the U.S. hockey team's accomplishment triggered a national celebration, the injury to figure skater Randy Gardner brought a nation to tears during the 1980 Winter Games. Randy and Tai Babilonia were the reigning world champion figure-skating pair and favorites for the gold medal in Lake Placid. They were America's skating darlings and the nation was on a first-name basis and had a love affair with this dynamic skating pair. Tai and Randy had practiced together for 11 years, ever since they were in elementary school, but Gardner's severe groin injury during practice destroyed their anticipated golden Olympic moment. The pair of skaters could not compete as planned at the Olympic Arena. It was crushing to watch their warm-ups. Gardner fell three times and twice he failed to lift Babilonia over his head in one of their signature moves. Gardner told John Nicks, their coach, that he could not continue. "They had no options," Nicks told Tom Boswell of the Washington Post. "Randy really wanted to go on. But I had to withdraw them."

They became known as the heartbreak kids of Lake Placid. Both left the arena after the devastating warm-ups by a side door and were driven away. My job was to handle the press for this heartbreaking story. I had promised the media that I would get the coach, the doctor, the parents, but no kids. They were too devastated. That was the least I could do for Tai and Randy to ease their devastating disappointment.

Two reporters, Phil Hersh of the Chicago Tribune and Neil Amdur of the New York Times, decided they would go interview the skaters themselves. They tried to make their way down to the locker room to

Between news conferences and broken dreams, there were lighter moments at the Olympics. Ed arranged for close friend and cardiologist Gene Drago to be the doctor for ABC-TV. Gene relaxed here on the top of Whiteface Mountain – on an uninstalled toilet.

question the kids, but they didn't have the proper credentials to gain access because it was off-limits to the media. They decided to try to knock down the door. I got a call from security and went to the locker room. I told Hersh and Amdur: "Guys, you have a choice. You're going to get arrested or you can go upstairs to the news conference and hear from the mother and the father and the coach and the trainer and the doctor." Without argument, the two reporters retreated upstairs. They were trying to do their jobs and I was doing mine. We ended up becoming friends.

Another great friendship that developed in Lake Placid was with skater Scott Hamilton, who is a tremendous person. He finished fifth in men's singles in the 1980 Winter Games and went on to win the 1982, 1983 and 1984 gold medals at the World Championships and the gold medal at the 1984 Olympic Winter Games in Sarajevo. I had a lot of fun with Scott and both of us shared a similar sense of humor.

But Hamilton's childhood was not humorous. Adopted at the age of six weeks, he was two years old when he contracted a mysterious illness that caused him to stop growing. Initially, his disease was diagnosed as cystic fibrosis, and doctors gave him just six months to live. But cystic fibrosis was one of several misdiagnoses in his case. Finally, he was correctly diagnosed as having Shwachman–Diamond syndrome, or SDS, a rare congenital disorder that can result in bone marrow dysfunction, skeletal abnormalities, short stature and a number of other serious complications. He was expected to become an invalid, but at the age of nine, he began doing figure staking as therapy. "Instead of just helping me a little, I think it cured me," Hamilton said. "Skating got my muscles moving again. It just started everything in me living again."

He grew to be 5-feet 4-inches and 140 pounds, which meant he was the smallest member of the entire U.S. Winter Olympic Team. That fact made the honor he received – being selected by his fellow athletes to carry the American flag into the Opening Games Ceremony – all the more remarkable.

But before that tribute, his teammates tested Hamilton's great sense of humor. He had gone to see the movie, "Close Encounters of the Third Kind." During the film, several of his Olympic teammates walked into the theater. Ice dancer Stacy Smith said to him, "Scott, how could you do a terrible thing like that? How could you disgrace us all?" Another teammate said, "We just heard Scott. You've been kicked out of the Olympic Games. How could you get yourself expelled? It reflects on all the rest of us."

"They really had me scared," Hamilton recalled. "They had me convinced that I had broken some rule and had been thrown out."

They had taken the joke far enough and his teammates started laughing and told him the incredible good news: that he would be carrying the American flag. It was another golden Lake Placid moment we will never forget. Scott Hamilton is exceptional in many ways.

After turning professional, he toured with the "Ice Capades" for two years before creating "Scott Hamilton's American Tour," which morphed into "Stars on Ice." He also did skating commentary for network TV. Maureen and I ran into him regularly when we were on the ice skating circuit handling sponsorships, TV rights and press for the U.S. Figure Skating Association.

In my opinion, Scott Hamilton was one of the very few professional athletes that I knew who really gave back to the sport when he got on top. He was always willing to do things to help the sport or help kids. We were in Chicago to do a clinic at a public rink, and Scott was out there showing them how to fall down on the ice – with a big smile on his face.

A year ago, Scott was at the Cleveland Clinic at the same time as Marylou Whitney and John Hendrickson. In the VIP dining room, John introduced himself, and asked Scott if he knew me.

"Sure I know Ed Lewi. He wanted me to do some back flips at Rockefeller Center for the Today show. The rink was full of water. I could have killed myself. Ed Lewi nearly killed me."

Then Scott laughed. It was good to see his sense of humor has remained intact.

Chapter 30:
My Russian Spy Misadventure

Ed was convinced he was under surveillance by the KGB during his visit to Moscow for a meeting of the International Olympic Press Association. Geoff Miller, AP's London bureau chief and a frequent visitor to Moscow, helped Ed search for a concealed microphone in Ed's hotel room - with nearly lethal results. Geoff (tie intact) is pictured above with other IOC Press Commission member and Maureen.

ecause of our work handling press prior to the Winter Olympics, I was asked to attend a meeting of the International Olympic Press Association in Moscow. Maureen had too much work to do back at the office and decided she would rather hold down the home front. Besides, after her breaking and entering in Communist-controlled Prague, she was worried that she might have been on the KGB's Most Wanted list.

I wanted to look professional, so we put together 400 press kits that I intended to hand out to the 400 Press Association people at the conference. I miscalculated the level of scrutiny

and bureaucracy such a simple matter took in the Soviet Union many years before the fall of the Berlin Wall and the crumbling of Communism for good in Russia.

Since I was a guest of the Soviet government, I was met at the Moscow airport by folks who were described to me as PR people. They were courteous and spoke fluent English. Only they weren't PR people, as I soon discovered. My first hint was when they took great interest in the 400 press kits and decided that it was imperative that they examine each page of each one, intensely and carefully. This could take days. I guess they had me pegged for a spy.

The two men assigned to me began going through the first stack of press kits, line by line and page by page. This went on for more than an hour when I finally had enough. "They're all the same," I said. "Do we have to go through all through this?"

They insisted it was a necessary exercise.

I wondered what they expected I might do. Steal some important trade secret? I was certain that in advance the KGB had assembled a full dossier on me. I was a member of the International Olympic Press Committee so they had everything they ever wanted to know about Ed Lewi, that's for sure.

"They were paranoid, always paranoid," Maureen recalled. "We couldn't call them Russians. We had to call them Soviets."

They gave their approval to the press kits, but they had messed up the pages and I had to re-do and collate them all over again. This was a few more hours of drudgery for me that I could have avoided, but you don't argue with the KGB. That much I knew from watching spy movies.

I thought it was going to be smooth sailing ahead after my press kits passed the censors and had been given the green light. I was allowed to proceed to my hotel, with the minders accompanying me, of course. They gave me a key to my room with strict instructions that I was not to leave the floor without leaving the key with the floor lady. There also happened to be a hallway matron on each floor and these women looked like they may have been past champion shot putters for the East Germany Olympic team. I knew that I wouldn't want to have to fight any one of them. Besides their stern demeanor and imposing bulk, each one of them also spoke fluent English. Now, things were getting rather curious and suspicious, too. I've never been a conspiracy theorist, but this was more than random coincidence. I stayed put on my hotel floor and did not dare offend the linebackers in women's clothing – excuse me, the hallway monitors.

One afternoon, I had a conflict. I was scheduled to give a report on the progress of planning for Lake Placid, but a press boat cruise was planned for the same time on the Russian Riviera – hardly a Soviet oversight. I had committed to delivering the report and did so to the small audience. My buddy, Geoff Miller, an Olympics expert and bureau chief in London for the Associated Press, went to dinner with me.

It was nice to get off the floor in my hotel, which had started to feel like a kind of house arrest. Geoff and I enjoyed dinner and a few drinks and we returned to the hotel, convinced by the circumstantial evidence and our hushed dinner conversation – Geoff was a journalist who had visited Moscow often and he understood the Soviet system and mindset – that we were under surveillance by the KGB and that my hotel room had been bugged.

Geoff came with me back to my hotel room. We had a mission that we felt was possible rather than impossible. We were bound and determined to locate the surveillance device. We started hunting for the bug. We unscrewed light switches, got down on our hands and knees and searched under the bed and stood on chairs to inspect the molding around the room. We found nothing out of the ordinary. We rolled up an area rug in the middle of the room and we found a silver-colored, round plate with a screw that looked very suspicious. We were both convinced it had to be a hidden microphone. I pulled a coin out of my pocket and we used that as a screw driver and went to work dismantling the bug. "We've got it!" I declared with a tone of swagger. "We're going to show the KGB who's smarter. Let's get that screw out."

As I easily turned the coin in the slot of the screw, I remember thinking about how easily it turned and with a few spins, it was free. Only there was no tiny microphone to be pulled out. Instead, I heard a whooshing sound, followed by a deafening crash as the chandelier that I had just unscrewed dropped from the ceiling beneath our feet directly to a wooden floor below. The glass exploded into tiny little pieces as it exploded with such weight after a free-fall of about 16 feet – since the ceilings were especially high.

I think my heart skipped a beat and the blood drained from my face. I thought I had just killed a room full of Soviets. Miraculously, the room right below the chandelier was empty. I could look through the hole that was left when I unscrewed the weight-bearing chandelier plate and there was nobody rushing to the scene in the room. I got scared and freaked out a little bit. From what I had heard that if you got sent to a Soviet gulag you are never heard from again. I envisioned a life of being forced to do hard labor, breaking rocks or something, in a Soviet prison.

I was snapped out of my racing mind by a knock on the door. I told Geoff I was going to climb out a window and try to escape. He told me to calm down and went to answer the door. Luckily, it wasn't the KGB coming to arrest me. It was just our matronly hallway monitor. She was not smiling. Then again, she never smiled.

"Do you know you just broke the chandelier?" she asked.

"Yes, but I saw a loose screw and thought I was tightening it," I replied. Before she could say anything more, I said that I would be happy to pay for any damages.

"No," the matron insisted. "No, no. You're our guests."

I did not get hauled off to a Soviet gulag, did not get arrested or sent off to jail. It was never mentioned again, although Geoff will not let me forget the incident and neither will Maureen. I am certain that my file at the KGB had a new addendum added to it about the chandelier misadventure. I was happy I lived to tell the tale and that nobody was injured in my effort to find the bug. Although I didn't find a microphone, I am still convinced that I was being secretly recorded in my hotel room. Just because I was paranoid doesn't mean I was wrong.

***

Chapter 31:
The Bear Essentials

Ed was a master at using trained bears to promote products, including hawking newspapers for Hearst Corp.: Times Union, Knickerbocker News & Union-Star. Bears were an even bigger marketing draw than babes, Ed learned early on, and he hit promotional paydirt here with a bear willing to sell newspapers in downtown Albany.

I blame my friend and Times Union colleague Barney Fowler, city editor, and later a popular columnist, for one of my craziest moments and my favorite picture from a 40-year career as a P.R. man. The photo shows me with a huge grin, riding in a convertible with Maureen alongside a very large, very friendly (he was also smiling) black bear.

Barney convinced me to accompany the bear and its handler to a State Police trooper party. I helped secure the services of the bear through my friendship with Charley Wood and his Storytown U.S.A. theme park in the Adirondacks. The party turned out to be a bear of an event, pun intended. The big, shaggy-haired fellow seemed to like me. He put his baseball mitt-sized paw around my shoulder at one point and Maureen went along for the ride. It was a beary, beary tender moment. We bonded, the bear and I. It turned out to be the money shot for this book's cover, as well.

That wasn't the only time I employed a black bear. There was nothing like the incongruous sight of a trained bear undertaking a human endeavor to get people to stop what they were doing and to sit up and take notice. One of my early and most popular promos during my days at the newspaper was hiring a bear to hawk the Times Union and Knick News in downtown Albany. Luckily, he was an old and placid bear and I didn't have to worry about him getting loose or mauling passersby. Plus, his handler kept the bear on a tight leash with a heavy-duty chain. I got a lot of good press, even from competitors, sold a lot more papers than usual and turned many heads. I can attest that everyone smiled those times that I hired a bear to sell papers along North Pearl Street. It didn't hurt my reputation, either, as a promoter who knew how to think outside the box.

Sometimes, you couldn't blame me for creature discomforts, because a particular animal for a promotion was not my idea and mascots were thrust upon on me occasionally. Such was the case with Ronnie the Raccoon, the official mascot of the 1980 Olympic Winter Games. Others came up with this one, but I had to live with Ronnie,

literally. The raccoon's permanent home was at the zoo in Utica, N.Y., but Maureen and I became his legal guardians in Lake Placid. (Did I mention that my wife is a saint?) Ronnie the Raccoon had a large cage in our house in Lake Placid so there was less travel time when we needed to produce the critter for public relations events.

We got a request from ABC-TV before the Olympics that the network wanted Ronnie and the Utica zoo director to appear on "Good Morning America." ABC sent a chartered plane from New York to pick up the animal and its handler in Utica and booked them a room at the famous Plaza Hotel.

I was accompanying them to the GMA studio the next morning, so the zoo director and I went out to dinner the night before the show and left Ronnie, normally a docile raccoon, in the bathroom of the director's hotel room with some water in the tub so he could drink, splash and play when we were gone. We removed loose items including towels, soap and scale and made sure the bathroom was basically empty. We returned after a couple of hours to find the bathroom trashed. Ronnie had torn open a dozen or so rolls of toilet paper stored under the sink and must have had quite a party unrolling, shredding and tossing them. The bathroom looked like the inside of a cotton candy machine. Only it was toilet paper. Luckily, Ronnie didn't chew up any walls or bathroom fixtures and after an hour or so, we had the mess cleaned up and managed not to get ourselves booted from the Plaza.

That's the thing with animals, I've learned. Even the supposedly well-trained and tame ones can get a little stir-crazy when you least expect it. They are beasts of the wild, after all.

Chapter 32:
MIA Price Chopper Cadillac

How do you drop a Cadillac? Well, you've got to be very strong and tall and clumsy. Or, leave it to one of our incomparable promotions with WRGB-TV and Tim Welch, their former weather forecaster. This one didn't quite work out the way we anticipated, not unlike Manzini's not-so-great escape in Lake George. In the end, it wound up creating more publicity than any of us could ever have imagined.

Tim Welch frantically searched for the winner of a Cadillac he accidentally dropped into this pile of entries.

Price Chopper was one of our first clients and we represented them for nearly three decades before we ended our contract amicably.

We helped the Golub family take what had been the modest Central Market grocery stores to the next level as the Price Chopper chain with 24-hour supermarkets and a devoted and loyal hometown customer base. "We wanted to be local and give back to the community," said Chairman of the Board Neil Golub, the former President and CEO. "Ed had a lot of ideas. He was very creative. Ed was always one of those guys asking, 'How do I attract a crowd? How do I get attention? How do I do something people enjoy?' "

With the help of our firm, Price Chopper hosted a series of major community events, including Saratoga Fair at Saratoga Race Course and a Saratoga Performing Arts Center celebra-

tion that featured a monster-sized cake and drew thousands of attendees. We developed and promoted Price Chopper's signature community event, sponsorship of the major July 4th fireworks display at the Empire State Plaza that draws upwards of 40,000 people.

Of course, nobody has a perfect record and the inaugural Price Chopper Hot-Air Balloon Race at the New York State Fair in Syracuse was not my finest moment as a promoter. We had been using a hot-air balloon with the Price Chopper name and logo for advertising and I thought it would be great to have a balloon race from Syracuse to Albany's Washington Park. I figured it would be a big success, a can't-miss promotional opportunity.

We did not properly calculate the

prevailing wind direction that week, of east to west. This caused problems. There were days of delays from the announced start because the winds were not in our favor. Finally, the balloons went aloft, but only traveled a short distance before poor winds and weather problems forced them to descend. I remember that Syracuse police started getting calls from concerned citizens, including one elderly woman who apparently had vision problems or a fertile imagination, or both, that there were Martians landing at Syracuse University. No kidding. That's how the cops took the call. They were not pleased when they tracked the source of the airborne invasion. I expected I might get hauled off to jail in handcuffs.

Luckily for us, Neil understood the fickle nature of the winds and weather issues, he did not blame us and we were able to laugh it off and to continue working for Price Chopper.

Of course, a slight problem like a scratched hot-air balloon race did not deter me. For the record, we organized and promoted successful hot-air balloon races from Saratoga to Albany later in our careers. And Neil Golub continued to give me free rein when it came to promotions.

I remember one in particular, an early 1980s collaboration with WRGB-TV, Channel 6. We cooked up a wildly popular promotion to give away 10 Cadillac automobiles. We enjoyed weeks of excited build-up and great anticipation, which resulted in a spike in grocery sales and a spike in ratings for Channel 6.

The fantastic finale for the promotion was to be a live grand prize drawing at Saratoga Race Course in the winner's circle. The host for the made-for-TV event was WRGB's popular weather forecaster, Tim Welch.

The promotion drew a staggering number of entries that filled a flatbed truck for the big public drawing. Everything was going wonderfully and we had a big hit on our hands. We were basking in the glow of a runaway success. Standing in the sea of entries, Welch reached in and pulled out the first nine winners, and read their names and addresses flawlessly. The crowd went wild each time a new winner was called. This went on for quite awhile and it built to a crescendo for the final winning entry. But just after he read the 10th and final winner's first name, he inexplicably dropped that entry back into the enormous pile. He tried to make a joke of it. "I can't believe I dropped that," he told his viewers. He tried to hide a look of stunned disbelief. Our faces turned ashen, too. Welch ad-libbed, "Anyway, it's in here somewhere."

Somewhere was the operative word. It was worse than trying to find a needle in a haystack. Maureen took charge, of course. She yelled out: "Don't move!" We hoped that the 10th winning entry had landed and settled near Welch's feet. It had not. It fell back into the giant pile of scraps of paper and looked the same as all the others. The only thing we had to go on was a generic-sounding first name, a hometown of Rotterdam and a certain style of handwriting that Tim felt he could recall if he saw it again. We were paralyzed with fear. What the hell were we going to do now? I restrained myself from throttling Welch. I liked the guy, but he had just made an epic fumble. From Tim's description, our office staff searched the bagged entries that were near Tim's feet for more than a week.

Luckily, Neil Golub came up with a practical solution. Price Chopper struck up a deal with the Rotterdam Senior Citizens to have its members go through the losing entries, which were trucked to the senior center in large garbage bags. In exchange for the mundane menial labor of sorting through the entries and looking for the 10th winner, Price Chopper agreed to pay for a new refrigerator for the kitchen at the Rotterdam Senior Citizens Center. It was a win-win situation and a nice way to get us all out of an embarrassing gaffe.

Every night on the 6 p.m. and 11 p.m. WRGB newscast, Welch or one of the anchors gave a brief update. This went on for days as the search continued, and the story spread regionally and then went national. At long last, one of the women at the senior center found it. The ticket was verified by Welch and the winner was contacted. She turned out to be a very deserving winner, a resident of a trailer park in Colonie, but the search process took so long that the senior center got a full kitchen out of the deal.

Price Chopper scored a big win, too. Neil Golub was out at the Dinah Shore Open golf tournament in Palm Springs, California and he turned on the TV in his hotel room and saw the story on the national news. He couldn't have gotten that kind of publicity at any price. Neil forgave me the dropped Cadillac and the hot-air balloon race fiasco, probably because I always admitted when I'd made a mistake and it normally ended up with a flood of unexpected publicity, often on a national scale.

"It turned out to be a lot of fun," Golub said of the years we represented Price Chopper. "I've got very good memories from Ed Lewi."

***

Chapter 33:
Aruba & "The Real Mrs. Lewi"

Ed & Maureen's involvement in the 1980s in Divi Resorts, a Caribbean island hotel chain, was one of their happiest, most carefree adventures. They made dozens of trips to Aruba and other islands and enjoyed what Ed dubbed "barefoot elegance."

When Maureen accompanied me for the first time to the resort in Aruba where I was a partner, it was well known by the folks at the resort that Maureen was not the first female acquaintance there I had brought.

Maureen and I started dating after I got involved with Divi Aruba. The Divi front desk registered me and my previous dates as Mr. and Mrs. Lewi. But after several trips there with Maureen, they could see that Maureen and I were such a great match that they started calling Maureen "The Real Mrs. Lewi." The name stuck.

From Maureen's perspective, our Aruba phase was the most fun we've ever had during a long and happy marriage and an exciting professional career together.

This grand adventure for us began when I met a man in the bar at the Desmond Hotel, near the airport in Colonie. The guy's name was Wally Wiggins and he was an energetic, enterprising lawyer in Ithaca, New York, who had a dream to build a resort hotel on the Caribbean island of Aruba. This was in the late-1960s. I was working in advertising at the Times Union and Wally wanted me to invest in a 30-room hotel under construction in Aruba. I told him I didn't have the cash to be an investor, but I'd like to visit the place. I'd never even heard of Aruba at that point. But Wally bought me a plane ticket and I spent time in Aruba for the first time. I fell in love with the sandy beaches, friendly people and incredible weather. It was a tropical paradise. I didn't wear shoes the whole time I was there. The island was so mellow they didn't even bother with locks on the doors of the hotel.

Eventually, I scraped together a modest amount of money and decided to become an investor because I thought the property was extraordinary and very special. After Maureen and I got married and I took her down to Aruba for the first time, we agreed to invest more in Wally's dream. The name, Divi Resorts, came from the unusual native trees there. During our time involved, Divi Resorts grew in the 1970's and 1980's into the largest hotel chain in the Caribbean with hotels in Aruba, Nassau, Antigua, Bonaire, Cayman Brac, St. Martin, Barbados and St. Croix.

Wally's original plan to build a single hotel in Aruba grew to 18 hotels on 14 islands and it got so big that that we had no choice but to take it public and to sell shares of stock in order to fuel the costly expansion plan.

We came to think of ourselves as the biggest and dumbest investors simultaneously. We sold pieces of the company to junk bond dealers after going public and what seemed like a shrewd idea at the time turned disastrous. The sad ending to the story is that we all went bankrupt with a company with more than $125 million in financial obligations – namely, construction bond

debt — and nowhere near that much in revenue and assets to cover us. In the end, the bond holders wound up with a controlling interest of Divi Resorts. They asked me to rejoin the new board and despite protests from Maureen, I decided to sign on again because I thought Divi was too special not to be involved.

Maureen chided me for being a romantic and believing in a renaissance for Divi, which I had branded through marketing and promotions as a resort of "barefoot elegance."

Because of rapid stock price increases, splits and the intermittent sale of blocks of our personal stock over the years, we were lucky that Maureen and I never lost a dime on Divi. We both look back on that chapter with utmost affection and the realization that it was a marvelous adventure we would never regret. "Divi and all the islands made up one of the greatest times of our lives," Maureen said. "We went to the Caribbean frequently. It was a getaway. It was very informal. We'd go to meetings in our swimsuits."

Our marketing approach was grassroots instead of advertising in the New York Times. Pilots needed a place to stay over. We worked with American Airlines, then with other airlines. We would give the pilots extra goodies, like hibachis for cookouts. We had other ideas that worked, such as giving away trips as prizes on TV game shows. Business was good and we had a great time vacationing in Aruba and with our Divi adventure.

***

Chapter 34:

Pulling Off a White House Stunt

Only Ed would join in a promotional stunt to fly Santa Claus and reindeer to the White House to entertain underprivileged children at an annual holiday party. The only problem was that they weren't exactly invited and yet showed up anyway.

My use of animals to gain attention for promotions and special events took me to the most exclusive addresses, including 1600 Pennsylvania Avenue NW in Washington, D.C. The White House caper grew out of an idea that Harold Fortune had to have reindeer fly in on a plane to the White House to entertain underprivileged children who came for a holiday party to the presidential home around Christmas each year. Harold tapped me to help him with the special promotion.

Mobil Oil had a DC-9 retrofitted so that it could carry a herd of reindeer.

I had a few problems with reindeer in the past and luckily no reindeer got loose on the way to the White House. A short distance away, we hooked up the reindeer to a sleigh, loaded in Santa Claus and gifts, and arrived at the gate of the White House. Unfortunately, we had not done all the advance planning and clearance checks called for. In fact, we were winging it. The guard checked the official visitors' list and did not see Santa and his reindeer on it, not to mention two husky public relations guys. The guard denied us entrance.

I tried everything I knew to change the guard's mind and let us in. This pleading, cajoling and haranguing went on for 90 minutes or so. Nothing budged him. I went for broke. "Maybe we could hold a press conference to say that President Reagan is barring a visit from Santa Claus to the White House," I suggested in my sweetest voice.

Bingo. I finally struck a nerve and the gate opened. Santa, the reindeer, Harold and I went onto the White House lawn. Out stepped Nancy Reagan, who was gracious and shook everyone's hand and thanked us for coming. The meet-and-greet was over in about 60 seconds. And then the First Lady went back inside.

We were not invited to follow her. An aide ushered us back to the gate and my White House visit was history, but we left with great photos and bragging rights about taking Santa to the White House.

***

Chapter 35:
Our Greatest Food Bloopers

When bears and babes lost their luster, Ed knew how best to appeal to consumers: through their stomachs. He used all manner of food at promotional events to both delicious and hilarious effect.

Animals were an unpredictable prop for promotions and so, I learned, was food. I thought I had come up with a great idea for a fundraiser for the Albany Medical Center: A Jello slide. No kidding. I knew I could pull it off I got permission from the state Office of General Services, who are in charge of all events at the Empire State Plaza. OGS officials gave me permission to set up a Jell-O slide as long as I cleaned it all up afterward. I agreed.

I found a large portable pool, equipped with a slide and got my staff to help set it up outside on the Empire State Plaza, near the reflecting pool and close to the Egg. We filled the pool with strawberry Jell-O – it took so many pounds of the mix that I lost count – and stirred it up good and let it set up. It was nice and jiggly by the time the fundraiser started. We charged $5 for each person who wanted to slide into a pool of strawberry Jell-O – including a mouthful of Jell-O if the person did a face plant.

It was very popular. More than 100 people forked over $5 each and did the Jell-O slide. Some people thought it was so much fun and they did it more than once. The faint of heart merely handed over donations to support the hospital. It was a hot, sunny day and we had a big crowd around the Jell-O slide. There was a lot of whooping and laughing and picture-taking.

Of course, there was one person who didn't listen to the rules. This big guy sidestepped the slide and did a belly flop into the pool. I'm not sure if he was intoxicated, but he ended up fracturing his ankle. He was in pain and quite upset and yelled that I would have to pay for it. I told him he didn't follow the rules. Before we came to blows, a hospital official stepped in and said the hospital would put it in a cast free of charge. That wasn't good enough for this yahoo. He informed me he was going to sue me. I informed him there was a long line of litigants in front of him and he'd have a long wait until his turn came around. That worked.

But there was a post-script. TV reporter John McLaughlin, an old friend of mine from our days working together at the Times Union, called our house. He was laughing. He said the Albany police got a report of a red substance flowing into the Hudson River. They investigated, could not determine what it was, and called the Coast Guard because they feared it might have been a dangerous pollutant. McLaughlin stopped cracking up long enough to tell us that they'd figured out that the Jell-O was dumped into a nearby sewer drain and eventually turned to a liquid and emptied through a drainage pipe in the river. "You guys have got to come down here," McLaughlin said with a chortle. "You really have to see the walleyes gulping down the strawberry Jell-O." We avoided arrest and were given a simple reprimand. What I wanted to say was that it was all-natural and the fish loved it. No harm, no foul, right?

Another one of our food ideas was to give away a slice of apple pie in a small container to patrons as they

entered the Saratoga Performing Arts Center for a concert titled "A Night of American Music." You know, as American as apple pie. It just popped into my head.

We thought we had the perfect promotional item. But I didn't remember to include a fork. I had not thought of that small detail and nobody caught the omission beforehand.

"You should have seen the audience trying to eat apple pie with their fingers," SPAC President Herb Chesbrough said in a story in the Capital District Business Review.

My food adventures were just beginning. I remembered to provide spoons, at least, for annual ice cream eating contest we organized at Saratoga Race Course each summer during track season to promote Stewart's Shops, one of our best promotional partners at the track. "We've been doing business with Ed for more than 30 years ago," Bill Dake, Stewart's chairman of the Board said. "We did a lot of civic activities and promotions with him. Ed has this constant pursuit of doing something new. He could generate ideas, but more importantly, he was effective in getting other people to get ideas. For every idea he had, I'd bet money that he got somebody to think of two or three of their own, and that's no small skill."

Starting in 2000, the company sponsored "Stewart's Day at the Races" and came up with a new flavor at the start of each racing season. The first new flavor was Hunch Crunch. Others included Funny Cide Pride, named after the 2003 New York-bred that captured both the Kentucky Derby and Preakness Stakes that year. There was also Choco Jocko Bailey for Saratoga's all-time leading rider and Hall of Famer Jerry Bailey. There was also Finish Line Fudge, Coffee Chocolate Exacta and Muddy Track.

The first annual Stewart's ice cream

contest was held in 2006 and there were three age groups: under 12, 12 to 18, and older than 18. They were very popular contests and a lot of fun to run. Who doesn't love eating free ice cream?

We had a good run with Tom Mailey, Stewart's marketing manager. "Ed's always got that creative thing going on inside his head," Mailey said. "He always has that one last thought. Sometimes, it's crazy."

Crazy does not always translate to a successful venture. I thought it would be great to get the winning horse of the featured race on "Stewart's Day at the Races" to sample Stewart's ice cream in the winner's circle. Nobody explained this to the horse. Despite the efforts of the winning jockey, Jerry Bailey, he could not convince his winning horse to eat ice cream. Afterwards, Dinny Phipps, the president of the Jockey Club and former Chairman of the New York Racing Association, gestured to me to come over to see him. "That's the first time I ever saw you fail," he said with a smile. I took that as a great compliment, coming from a pretty remarkable man in the horse racing industry and beyondGetting a horse to eat ice cream may have been beyond my capabilities, but I fared better with a giant cake baked by Price Chopper to celebrate an important anniversary for the Saratoga Performing Arts Center. Finally, after 24 hours of preparation and baking, the humongous cake was iced, decorated and trucked to the track.

Price Chopper President and CEO Neil Golub gave the giant cake a thumbs up. "It was huge. Monster-sized," he said. I figured the cake was three stories high (about 60 feet) and roughly 40 feet wide. More than 5,000 people who attended a SPAC concert each got a nice slice of cake, after nearly an hour of cutting and plating. The

first ceremonial piece went to Golub and I made sure to taste a piece right away. It was terrific. There was one glitch. Neil Golub apparently slipped. I didn't see it. But I saw the big gouge in the cake, caused by him falling into it. It was a bit embarrassing, but Golub was a good sport about it. He tasted some of the icing that was smeared all over his shirt, jacket and tie. Let them eat cake, Ed figured. At least this time he remembered to bring the forks.

That's not all, though. We prepared a giant cookie for Funny Cide Day at Saratoga, when the fan favorite and New York-bred winner of both the 2003 Kentucky Derby and Preakness Stakes was honored. Originally, the ideas was to bake a cake (smaller than the monster-sized cake that Neil Golub fell into) in the shape of a key to the city of Saratoga Springs. There were a lot of failed attempts and it was decided the shape was too difficult. "As an alternative, after we checked with Funny Cide's trainer Barclay Tagg to make sure the ingredients were suitable for his horse. I got our friend Angelo Mazzone, owner of 677 Prime, the Glen Sanders Mansion and other upscale restaurants, to make a giant cookie in the shape of a key to the city full of molasses and grains that the horse liked. "They spent hours making that cookie," recalled Mark Bardack, senior vice-president of our firm at the time. "It was gorgeous and contained everything the horse liked to eat.

NYRA CEO and President Charlie Hayward and Funny Cide's jockey, Hall of Famer Jose Santos, presented the cookie to Funny Cide. "He took a great big bite out of it," Bardack said. "It was a great photo-op."

And that's the way the cookie crumbles and with that lame pun, we'll move on from the food incidents to other fun stories that don't involve animals or recipes.

Chapter 36:
More Celebrity Encounters

Ed Lewi Associates worked with several celebrity clients. Ed and Maureen often squired them around Saratoga Springs during summer visits. Merv Griffin hired the firm to promote radio stations he bought in Albany. Here, Ed jokes with Griffin and Eva Gabor during a tour of the Saratoga Race Course

We have met and worked with a wide range of celebrities but some of our experiences with celebrities have been, to say the least, unorthodox. Consider the time that we ended up eating chicken at Boston Market in Saratoga Springs with Merv Griffin, Eva Gabor and Donald Trump – in black tie and formal gowns, no less. Merv hired Ed Lewi Associates to promote the radio stations he bought, WTRY and WPYX in Albany and WPOP in Hartford, Connecticut. Griffin and Gabor visited Saratoga one summer to check in on his radio stations and enjoy a brief getaway.

He asked me to plan some activities for them and to get them invited to any gala events that were being held when they were in town. The National Museum of Dance turned out to be a disaster that particular year. They hung heavy décor drapes and cut off the air-conditioning. The food was late and underwhelming when it finally arrived. The guests were sweating profusely and complaining loudly. Several people bailed out. Donald Trump was there with his wife Marla. Trump pulled me aside and asked, "Is there a fast food place around here?" I told him there was a Boston Chicken up the Street and said that I'd be happy to take him. He invited Merv and Eva to come along. I joined Merv and Eva and Donald and Marla. We made quite an entrance to the fast-food place pulling up in limos, in our tuxedoes. There was whispering as our group walked up to the counter to order. People started coming over to ask for autographs and they obliged.

Ed had several occasions to meet and work with Bob Hope, who performed at the Colonie Theater in Latham, the Saratoga Performing Arts Center and the Saratoga Fair, which was held at Saratoga Race Course in 1974 and 1975. The rationale behind the Saratoga Fair was sound: get some use out of the vacant Saratoga Race Course before the racing meet started. Some promoters came from Chicago. The locals got very excited because they said they could get Bob Hope. NYRA (the New York Racing Association) was involved because they owned the facility. The group from Chicago handled the bookings. I did a lot of press work.

Hope and his wife, Delores, were terrific. Bob was great because he was congenial and was happy to get involved in community events when he was in town. He'd write a check or tape a public service announcement for charities. Bob and Delores were first class folks all around. They were just as nice off-camera as on-camera, which is rare.

Someone who was much different in person from their public persona was Joan Rivers, the popular comedienne. We saw first-hand that Joan is actually a very shy person. She is a great friend of Marylou's and John's and we all had dinner with her before her show at the Colonie Theater. We had purchased our tickets but she suggested that she didn't want us to see her show. "I don't want you to go because that's not me," she told us. "That's just a part I play. It's what I do for a living, but that's not really me as a person." Out of respect for Joan, we gave away our tickets and didn't go to the show.

Many years ago, we took Ron Rickles and his wife, Barbara, out to dinner at the former Stone Ends restaurant in Albany. I was going out with a girlfriend from Chicago at the time and Rickles insisted that he wanted to marry us that night. "You can't marry them," his wife quipped. "you don't even know them."

Some of the others we got to know included Liza Minnelli, Frank Sinatra, Liberace, Sammy Davis, Jr., Englebert Humperdinck, Susan Lucci and Michael Jakcson. I asked Susan Lucci, the soap opera star, to be grand marshal of the Belmont Stakes Festival Parade in Garden City. It was near her hometown, local residents loved her and they went wild when they spotted her. "I never had that experience before," Susan said and she was genuinely touched and emotional about the outpouring of love by her hometown folks.

Liza Minelli was a lot of fun, too. She was great to her fans who waited for a long time in a long line to get her autograph. The only celebrity I saw who spent more time signing autographs was Liberace. Liza made everyone in the audience feel like they were the most important person in the world. She had a great rapport with the crowd that was wonderful to see.

***

Chapter 37:
Like Father, Like Sons

Ed's sons, Joe, left, and Jim enjoyed extraordinary access to celebrities and special events growing up and both ended up working in the entertaining industry, influenced by their father's career.

My sons, Joe and Jim, who are now in their 40s, did not have a typical childhood growing up. While other kids were immersed in Little League, my boys were attending promotional events and rubbing shoulders with celebrities. They had a front-row seat for real-life lessons in media relations, marketing and public relations. "We were slave labor to my Dad," Jim recalled with a laugh. "We were collating and stapling press releases." The only times the boys got really upset was when we had them play Raggedy Ann and Andy and dress as elves to be in the Christmas parade in Schenectady.

Indentured servitude had its perks, though. The Lewi boys regularly got to hang out backstage at SPAC. Joe's favorite story involves Michael Jackson and the Jackson 5 concert at SPAC. "I was about 10 years old at the time and Michael was about 12," Joe recalled. "He was showing us how to play the piano. It was my brother and me and Michael and his brother. After we played the piano for awhile, it was time for the Jackson brothers to have dinner before their concert. They invited us to go with them to the green room, a backstage area for VIPS. We all dug into buckets of Kentucky Fried Chicken."

"When you're young, meeting a

rock star or a celebrity is a big deal," Jim said. "My friends were very impressed. My friends thought my parents were cool. Some of them would get paid to work for them at their consumer shows. When we were young, we loved being around show business."

"Our dad and mom were always busy," Jim said. "They worked all the time. They taught us how to make a good living and how to have a good work ethic."

Both Joe and Jim were influenced by what they saw growing up and ended up going into the promotion and entertainment business. Joe went to work right after college with the Ringling Bros. and Barnum & Bailey Circus as a marketing manager. "Ringling Brothers hired me because they knew I grew up with P.R. and promotions and knew what it was all about," Joe said. He worked for eight years with the circus and traveled widely. "I was on the road for 320 days a year. One of the first cities I was assigned to was Glens Falls. The P.R. firm was Ed Lewi Associates. One of the first checks I had to write was to Ed Lewi Associates. I don't know if my father cashed it. I loved it. I still relish the days I worked there."

Joe has developed a new business by combining his passion for cooking and the entertainment business. "You can't make any money being a cook my parents told me," Joe recalled. But in his late 40s he went to culinary school in Boston and became a chef.

"Now I feel I've been able to do both things I wanted to do. I'm teaching, and I started my own business because cooking was always a passion with me. I'm trying to meld my two worlds together a little bit. I'm trying to create a culinary/entertainment business."

Joe and his wife, Melissa, have two teenage children and live in Natick, Massachusetts. His younger brother, Jim, lives in Los Angeles. He and his wife, Lori, have two teenage girls.

While at Ithaca College, Jim managed a band and also worked as a stagehand. After graduation, he worked with Jon Zazula, who managed Metallica. "I got to go on tour with Metallica and it was great," he said. He now heads his own company, LiveWorks, which handles all aspects of developing and producing concerts and events. He also serves as a consultant for entertainment companies. "I'm trying to be multifaceted," he said. "My father has so many ideas and wants to do so much, and he has a good heart," Jim said. "He wants to be around where the action is. We benefited from that and I learned everything about the entertainment business from him."

"I don't think my father's career was something you can learn," Joe said. "It's natural. He has a great instinct for what will work. You either have it or you don't. He's always had that burning desire to do something more. He loves those challenges. He's very competitive and he loves to win, to see things succeed."

***

Chapter 38:
Secret to Success: Marry Well

Ed and Maureen host a wedding party for hundreds of guests aboard the Ticonderoga during a Lake George cruise with a Mardi Gras theme, as well as circus acts and fireworks. They'll celebrate their 40th anniversary in 2015.

I can pinpoint the moment when my career in marketing and public relations began to take off. It's no mystery that the secret to my success is my better half. The greatest thing that ever happened to me was when I married Maureen. It was 1975, four decades ago, and the time has raced by. Thanks to Maureen, it's been not only a wild ride, but a wildly happy one, too.

Our good friend, Liz Bishop, anchor on WRGB, Channel 6, likes to needle me that I am 13 years older than Maureen and Liz often reminds me how hard Maureen works. "She didn't get a marriage license when she married you, it was more like a work permit," Liz

likes to joke.

Maureen and I have very different working styles and yet we make a great team and continue to work together in harmony after almost 40 years. Friends have their theories. "Maureen watches the pennies. Eddie is the idea guy and she puts it to work," John Hendrickson said. "Ed, like me, is scattered. He goes on to the next thing while someone is cleaning up from the previous one. It's worked brilliantly. What's great about Ed and Maureen is they're not just business partners; they're not just marriage partners, they're best friends. They do everything together."

There is, of course, a back story to our union. Both Maureen and I lost our first spouses by death when each of us was just 29 years old. Friends were trying to be helpful and offered to fix us up on a blind date, but Maureen didn't want anything to do with me and the feeling was mutual.

So many friends were trying to get us together for a date that we finally relented, although Maureen had a boyfriend in Florida at the time and I was dating a woman in Chicago. We met for dinner and it went so badly that we both assumed it would be our first – and our last – date together.

I don't know why, but I found myself asking her out to dinner again. Maureen agreed, and the chemistry improved. At the time, Maureen was working in the Albany law office of Howard Nolan, who was preparing to embark on a distinguished political career as a state senator for 20 years.

"There aren't too many people around as good as Maureen was," Nolan recalled. "She was terrific. I mean she had everything, including brains and personality. She was tops. She did my legal work; she helped me manage my real estate holdings and ran the office. She did everything."

Maureen and I later realized our paths had crossed a few months before our first date through a most unfortunate and nearly catastrophic ursine manner involving Nolan & Heller.

One afternoon, a guy off the street walked into the Nolan & Heller law office on State Street and told the receptionist he needed a lawyer. She asked why. "I was bitten by a bear on the corner of State and Pearl streets," he informed her.

The receptionist thought it was a prank, but he insisted it was true and he wouldn't leave without a meeting, so the receptionist asked Maureen to come out of her office to meet with the guy. Maureen asked to see the bite marks, but the man did not have any, so Maureen was dubious and sent him

on his way because she knew Nolan would not want to be bothered with such a bogus claim. "There are a lot of other lawyers on State Street," Maureen told him and sent him on his way. She later heard that another lawyer took the guy's bitten-by-a-bear case.

The matter did not come up again for several months, when Maureen and I were at dinner and I was trying to speed things up because I didn't want to be out late. I told her I had to be up very early to attend a pre-trial hearing. She asked me for details.

I launched into my story about using a bear as a stunt to hawk the Times Union newspaper downtown and there was this guy who got a little too close and seemed to want to provoke the bear. But the good news, I told Maureen -- the bear did not have any teeth or claws.

"Oh. My. God," Maureen said, nearly spitting out her wine and sputtering and staring at me incredulously. "That was you?"

She was shaking her head in disbelief and laughing and wondering what the hell she was getting into dating this guy who brought a bear to downtown Albany, albeit an old bruin with no teeth and no claws.

I beamed. Yes, I told Maureen, the bear idea was mine and what's more, in addition to achieving a spike in sales of the Times Union, my promotion raised money for charity because I set up a picture-taking promotion that turned out to be wildly successful.

Maureen just stared as I rambled on. They say opposites attract. Whatever it is, we are lucky we found each other.

In case anyone reading this book wondered, the Times Union bear that allegedly put the toothless bite on that litigious guy was not the same bear wearing a floppy felt hat on this book's cover that I drove around in a convertible for the sheer fun of it. I have worked with a whole clan of bears over the years. Maureen is such a good sport, she's hung around the bears I've hired and she's even consented to driving along with them. Lucky for me, she enjoys my skewed sense of humor.

"He was fun," Maureen said. "We've always had a saying: 'You work hard; you play hard.' That's what we always did."

Maureen admits there has never been a dull moment. "Never. Not even now when Ed is pushing 80 and so-called retired, Ed never slows down," she said.

There were serious issues to work out before we got married, about a year after that first blind date that did not go so well. Maureen had to reach a comfort level with my two boys from my first marriage, Joe and Jimmy,

who were 10 and seven, respectively, when Maureen came into my life. That's a tough age for kids and what made the situation even more challenging was that I had a live-in housekeeper, Mae Mae Edwards, who had developed a strong bond with the boys. Her two-year-old son, Adrian, had come to live with us and became like a little brother to my two sons. Jimmy told me, "I want you to marry Mae Mae." I tried to explain that I didn't love Mae Mae and that I loved Maureen and was going to marry her, but Jimmy cried and he and his brother were having a hard time imagining their lives with Maureen as their stepmother.

"We were little kids at the time, and we weren't fond of anyone my father was dating," Joe recalled. "What helped us all hit it off was when the four of us went to California on an

Ed and Maureen will celebrate their 40th anniversary in 2015.

amusement park tour vacation. They wanted to make sure my brother and me were okay with them getting married."

When we checked into our resort in San Luis Obispo, the clerk asked if we wanted one two-bedroom suite or two separate suites. The clerk assumed Maureen and I were husband and wife. "Are you kidding? They aren't even married," Jimmy shouted out in the lobby.

So, we were busted by the little squirt and two suites it was. The transition for the boys was easier and better than we imagined. Our worries seemed to fade away as they began bonding with Maureen on that California vacation trip. As far as they are concerned, she is their mom, the only one they really ever knew. We three boys realize that she is the family's glue.

When it came to planning our wedding, I plead guilty about letting my marketing experience take over. I didn't just want a boring, traditional wedding. I wanted something unique and with pizzazz that our guests would enjoy and remember. We settled on a late-night party on the cruise ship Ticonderoga on Lake George on June 14, 1975, a Saturday. We billed it as a mini-Mardi Gras and sent poster-sized, whimsical invitations to more than 200 guests.

Since organizing the cruise was all-consuming, we opted for a simple wedding on June 12, 1975, a Thursday evening, with Joey and Jimmy and a few family members officiated by a friend of ours who was a justice of the peace.

It was full steam ahead with the Mardi Gras cruise, though. As guests walked up the gangway to board the Ticonderoga, they were greeted by a ventriloquist and a marching band of Lilliputians on the dock. When everyone was on board, the cruise ship pulled away from the dock, accompanied by the booming accompaniment of a barrage of cannon fire from Fort William Henry. There was a variety of entertainment throughout the ship for our guests. There were circus acts from Ringling Brothers, a sketch artist, funhouse mirrors and games from Charley Wood's parks, two bands and enough food and drink to satisfy an army by famous caterer Joe Kulik, who regularly served celebrities, governors and legislators at Joe's delicatessen in Albany.

As the wedding party and cruise along the length of Lake George was coming to a close in the wee hours of the morning and we approached Sun Castle, Charley Wood's estate, I had arranged for a spectacular fireworks display shot from his property. With a volley of cannon fire to announce our departure from the dock and the rockets' red glare to welcome us back, you could say it was an explosive party, and you could say our marriage has been a blast in every sense of the word.

***

Chapter 39:
The Summer Place To Be

On the way to the Winners Circle on Travers Day 2004 when Birdstone won the Travers after upsetting Triple Crown contender Smarty Jones in the Belmont. Everyone was soaking wet. The clouds had opened up into torrential rain as premature darkness eerily set upon the track, as the race began. Not even downpours could dampen Marylou's love of Saratoga.

Of all the projects, promotions, special events and causes Maureen and I have been involved in over the years together, perhaps none has given us more satisfaction than helping to return some of the luster to the Saratoga Race Course.

The track was not always the golden brand it is today and not always "The Summer Place to Be." The quality of Saratoga's racing meet also was not considered the best in North America, if not the entire world, as it is now.

Old-timers will recall that in the mid-1960s, Saratoga's average attendance was about 15,000 on weekends and 10,000 on weekdays during the 24-day meet. Finally, the trend was reversed and track attendance made some gains in the late 1970s. The New York Racing Association hired Ed Lew Associates in 1978 and we worked hard to achieve the upward trend.

Racing expert and turf columnist Michael Veitch reminds his readers regularly that the high-water mark was in 2003, when the average daily attendance was 29,147 during a 36-day meet. Coincidentally, the advertising and promotion budget was at its peak in that same era and it was possible to market to western New York, Pennsylvania, New Jersey, Massachusetts and

Connecticut to spread the good word about the uniqueness of Saratoga, consistently ranked among the top thoroughbred race tracks in America.

Our greatest ally in the renaissance of Saratoga was Marylou Whitney, the Queen of the Spa City. "I'd do anything to promote Saratoga," she said. Even when I asked her to ride on an elephant into the Winner's Circle, Marylou was always game and never turned down one of my unorthodox requests. Her late husband, C.V. "Sonny" Whitney, a famous thoroughbred horse racing owner and breeder and Saratoga Springs stalwart, encouraged her. "Bring back Saratoga the way it used to be," he told her. She has devoted herself to fulfilling her husband's wish.

The elephant's ride was a little rough, so the next time I asked her for a favor – to promote Saratoga during an appearance on the hit TV show, "The Lifestyles of the Rich and Famous," with host Robin Leach – I got her a ride in a vintage automobile, Greta Garbo's Dusenberg that I borrowed from Charley Wood. It was a classic Dusseldorf open touring car. Marylou rode in the passenger seat for the show as it moved slowly up and down North Broadway as she offered commentary on the magnificent Victorian mansions, historic architecture and other noteworthy items about the summer residents who came here for the racing season.

"I was happy to do any of the press things that Ed asked me to do because we were all working to bring back Saratoga," Marylou recalled. "I kept inviting up some of my friends from Hollywood and the theater scene in New York City and Ed got the press to come and we got a lot of publicity for Saratoga that way. I kept bringing in more people and we made a lot of progress. I remember when we were talking about how far we had come and we said, 'Saratoga is the summer place to be.' It stuck. It's more than a slogan. It's true. Ed and Maureen helped make it happen. They are like my family. My grandchildren call him Uncle Eddie."

I recall that Marylou only complained once, despite the myriad of media outlets who followed her around during the racing meet. After spending four full days and most of the nights with NBC Nightly News, while entertaining a dozen houseguests, Marylou adamantly requested us to close out the feature, and send the crew back to New York.

Soon, others took notice, too. In 1999, Saratoga Race Course, a National Historic Landmark, was named by Sports Illustrated as the 10th best sporting venue in the world.

Many others besides Marylou were on the inside of the track's success.

"Ed and Maureen are an inherent part of Saratoga," former NYRA CEO and President Charlie Hayward said in November, 2011. "In Saratoga, they've had a huge impact."

Bill Nader, a former senior NYRA official who left in 2007 to become executive director of the Hong Kong Jockey Club, put it this way: "Ed's business was to cultivate long-lasting relationships built on a trust factor that he could improve your business through a variety of services. And, in the end, he would deliver the goods, even if he cooked up a half-whacked idea that would somehow work. It was a family-type business and Ed wanted you to be part of the family."

When Hayward joined NYRA in 2004, Ed Lewi Associates immediately scheduled a community lunch and meetings to introduce him to Saratoga officials. "That's the kind of sensibility they have," Hayward said. "That wasn't just happenstance. Ed had a real understanding, especially in terms of NYRA, that the track is really owned by the community."

Ed took that understanding of the community nature of the track to the next level. He initiated a community open house on the Sunday before the meet began. It became a summer staple and a big draw that attracts more than 15,000 fans each year with free admission, free parking, wagerless steeplechase races, backstretch tours, handicapping seminars, pony rides and dozens of other attractions. The popularity of the open house and other event-oriented promotions contributed to the fact that Saratoga's demographics are far different than other racetracks in North America. Saratoga enjoys attendance that is equally divided between men and women, compared to other tracks that skew heavily to older males. By comparison, Saratoga attracts a much younger audience than other tracks.

Certainly, there is more press coverage about Saratoga than at any other track in North America. "If we were to paint the Ladies Room, there would be five TV stations there," Hayward said. That's a legacy of all the groundwork laid by Ed Lewi Associates.

I started an annual pre-Saratoga press conference on a Monday in late June, four weeks before the track's opening day, which has become a kind of institution. It is covered by every media outlet within 100 miles of Saratoga and a lot of buzz is generated by announcing the souvenir giveaways and what's new for the season.

"I was shocked at the media response, which included live television. It was amazing," Nader recalled of his first pre-meet press conference.

Ed also amped up the interest in the popular Saratoga track giveaways, which have included T-shirts, baseball caps, umbrellas, travel bags items and

other collectible items with a Saratoga logo given away free with each paid admission. Giveaways created a new breed known as "spinners." These are the folks who pay admission, get a freebie, and spin right around through the turnstiles and pay admission again to get another freebie. It's common to see spinners carrying arms full of giveaways that they often later sell at exorbitant prices on eBay, the online auction site.

Of course, it helped that Ed Lewi Associates always brought in attractive woman women to model the giveaway apparel. "You'd have thought it was the Academy Awards," Nader marveled.

We also realized that every giveaway was a free advertisement for Saratoga. Caps and T-shirts with the track logo have been seen in photos from around the world. Maureen and I have seen folks jogging in or wearing a Saratoga T-shirt in Europe, Asia, the Caribbean and across the U.S. "A good giveaway is in the fabric of Saratoga," Hayward said with a smile.

We had a lot of fun with our Saratoga ads, including a legendary TV spot. Somehow, I convinced longtime NYRA announcer Tom Durkin and former New York Giants Football Coach Bill Parcells, who owns thoroughbred horses and a house in Saratoga Springs, to a humorous commercial. The concept, written by Tom, was to have Durkin instruct Parcells, a rookie announcer, in the finer points of calling a horse race. But Parcells had a hard time picking it up. He held his binoculars the wrong way and asked several dumb questions. Durkin tried to explain how important traditions are in Saratoga. Parcells said, "Football has traditions, too" as he dumped a giant cooler of Gatorade onto Durkin's head. "One take only, Ed," a drenched, green-tinged Durkin said. That's all we needed. It was an epic commercial that people still talk about.

Maureen and I knew how fortunate we were to have had NYRA as a client and to promote Saratoga, and we tried to give back as often as possible. We helped organize and publicize some jockey softball games to benefit the Disabled Jockeys Fund. Sheryl Schwartz and I chaired a new fundraiser called the Travers Celebration that lasted 10 years and raised more than $1 million for B.E.S.T. and several other local charities. We also joined forces with several other charitable causes during the Saratoga meet. That meant we worked closely with Jerry Bailey, Saratoga's Hall of Fame jockey, and his wife, Suzee. "Ed and Maureen were invaluable in helping Suzee raise money," Bailey said. "They always came through."

When I asked Bailey to do a meet and greet with a ballet star before a performance at the New York City Ballet to demonstrate the athleticism of ballet, he was happy to return a favor. "I was doing it for Ed because of all he had done for me," Bailey said. "He did a lot of nice things for us, including getting us SPAC concert tickets."

I guess I had a knack for creating unusual pairings that somehow worked, despite the seeming incongruous nature of a jockey and a ballet dancer, for instance. Another idea that drew some blank stares at first, but which proved to be a big success, was my plan to have Saratoga jockeys compete in a go-kart race at The Great Escape for charity. I made sure to schedule it for a Tuesday, dark day at the track and the only day the jockeys had off each week. We dubbed the charity race The Travers 900. "It was a whimsical idea of Ed's in 2003," Mark Bardack recalled. "We let the jockeys bring their families for the entire day and we treated them to lunch as well, provided they raced. These guys are competitive by nature. Wouldn't you know, one jockey, Jean-Luc Samyn, decided to get an edge. He paid his own way into The Great Escape that morning to practice on the go-kart track."

John Velasquez offered cash to remove the governor from his go-kart's engine – yes, we controlled the speed with those guys. We didn't want the jockeys to get hurt on a no-pay go-kart ride. The kicker was that five television stations did a piece on the race every year. The front page of the Times Union one year featured a big photo of jockey Jose Santos, who'd won the first two legs of the Triple Crown with Funny Cide earlier that year, laughing as he drove a go-kart. The amount of free publicity that Saratoga Race Course and The Great Escape received from yet another one of my crazy ideas made for another fun experience. It also generated a lot of laughs for a lot of people along the way, and you can't put a price on that.

***

Chapter 40:
Retirement: What's That?

LEWI, LEWI!
More Than A Power PR Couple

After he sold Ed Lewi Associates in 2010, nobody expected Ed to go quietly into retirement. Even at age 80 and facing serious health issues, Ed continues to work for his favorite charitable causes alongside Maureen.

Maureen and I sold Ed Lewi Associates to our executive vice president, Mark Bardack, in 2010. Anybody who knew me realized I was not the retiring type.

At the time of the sale, our client list included Alpin Haus, Citizens Bank, Dunkin' Donuts, Hannaford Supermarkets, 38 High Rock Condominium in Saratoga Springs, the Great Northeast Home Show, Living Resources, Mazzone Management Group, the New York Racing Association, Northeastern Fine Jewelry, Siena College Athletics, the Sports Foundation of the Capital Region, Stuyvesant Plaza, The Wesley Community in Saratoga and several others.

The sale made news and resulted in four retirement dinners and roasts on our behalf. After the parties finally subsided, Maureen worried about what I'd do with all my free time. I ruled out golf, since I was always lousy at it and a back injury ruled out that hobby. I also was never a big reader. Promotion and staging big events was my passion and I never really gave that up after we sold the firm. Gratefully, cutting-edge back therapy helped reduce the pain and improved my mobility.

After the sale, we left for our winter home in Naples, Florida. We reunited with our close friends, whom we dubbed "The Rat Pack." Our group was made up of a half-dozen couples who all met more than two decades ago after Charley Wood urged us to give Naples a try. "I want you kids to come to Naples," he said. He always called us kids.

"You mean Naples, Italy?" I asked.

"No," Charley said. "Naples, Florida."

Charley convinced us that buying a condo near his overlooking the Gulf of Mexico was a good buy and that it would appreciate in value. We started vacationing in Naples, although down time was scarce.

A group of couples our age moved into the condo at the same time, into second-floor units. We grew close. We created the Sunday open house and we all left our doors open and wandered among the movable party apartments. The Rat Pack was born.

The members are as free-spirited and fun-loving as we are. We specialized in crazy antics. For example, we had tacky parties where we challenged each other to come in outrageously tacky costumes and the host served tacky food, amid tacky decorations. We celebrated each other's birthdays and mine on New Year's Eve was always celebrated doubly.

Once, when our next-door neighbor, Bill Pinkerton, who owned a large company that leases computers to governments, celebrated a birthday we concocted a surprise. We rented a small plane that towed a huge banner behind it declaring "Happy Birthday S.O.B." The FAA was not amused and demanded that the pilot get formal FAA approval. "I told them the S.O.B. stands for 'Sweet Old Bill.' " They bought the ruse and Pinkerton's friends saw the giant banner for miles around and got a big kick out of it.

For a New Year's Eve party, the Rat Pack installed a disco mirror ball with blinking lights at the top of the building and had it lowered at midnight. The police switchboard lighted up. An elderly woman and others had called the cops to suggest Martians had invaded. We let the police in on the joke and they stuck around for dessert.

Recently, we brought the Rat Pack in a van with a hot pink sign to the Adirondacks for a few days of camping. We stayed at Marylou Whitney and John Hendrickson's Camp on a Point.

For one of my birthdays, Tom Pyle, the head of Amtrak in the Northeast, burst out of the top of a gigantic birthday cake wearing a bra.

Her Adirondack property is bigger than the state of Rhode Island, so they had no shortage of fun activities.

Since we had a less hectic schedule after the sale, we got a 3-month-old Labradoodle, which we called MJ. We had wanted to get a dog for years. Marylou and John became the dog's godparents and even sent a chauffeured limousine to take us to pick up the dog at Newark Airport.

Maureen and I are busier than ever. We were intensely involved with the planning and execution of the 150th anniversary of Saratoga Race Course in 2013, the 100th anniversary of Camp Chingachgook on Lake George and Ed remains active on the board of SPAC. The cause that remains closest to our heart is the Double H Ranch. "There isn't anything Ed wouldn't do for those kids," Sheryl Schwartz said. She is the wife of Barry Schwartz, former NYRA Chairman and Calvin Klein co-founder. We brought Sheryl onto the board of Double H. "It's just a very special place and it holds a special place in our hearts and especially Ed's," she said. "He has worked tirelessly and built a very impressive board. The ranch will forever be indebted for what Ed has done. He doesn't want any credit, but he deserves it."

I've slowed my volunteerism there somewhat because of wintering in Florida, but I still remain committed and Honorary Lifetime Founding Vice Chairman.

As I write this, Maureen and I are enjoying a much-needed rest over the winter at our home in Naples, Florida after the exhausting marathon in the summer of 2013 that was Saratoga 150. Although we sold Ed Lewi Associates and vowed we were retired, we were busier than ever and last summer agreed to help organize and plan the ambitious schedule of more than 200 promotions and special events, from May through September, to promote the 150th anniversary. It was a whirlwind, but it was fun to promote a place and institution we love dearly.

Maureen served as Events Chair of Saratoga 150 and I as Public Relations Chair. Among hits in a myriad of publications up and down the U.S. East Coast and West Coast, on AOL and Yahoo, plus at least a dozen magazines, Chris Carola of the AP wrote a long feature for the Associate Press that was distributed on the international wire and a dozen photographs of Saratoga were featured. The story hit big and we heard from folks as far away as New Zealand and Japan.

Maureen spent almost a year in planning the 150th Floral Fete with Co-Chair Marlene Okby and Marylou Whitney who served as honorary chair with her husband John Hendrickson. The Floral Fete became the centerpiece event of the five-month long celebration, drawing more than 40,000 people. I am not alone with ambitious ideas. Marylou previously had a Floral Fete theme for one of her annual balls and thought it would be an unusual way to celebrate the 150th by replicating the popular event of the late 1800s.

As we look forward to the 151st racing season and the summer of 2014, Maureen and I will be joining the annual circus that is Saratoga. As I said at the outset, I was born a hustler and came into this world in the midst of a party and I'm not about to stop now that I'm becoming an octogenarian.

In closing, I can say one thing for sure. The only certainty about our future is that our wild ride will continue. "God knows what he'll do next," Marylou Whitney said. "Whatever it is, it will be a lot of fun."